D1042285

HARMONY
in
MARRIAGE

by **Rev. LELAND FOSTER WOOD, Ph.D.**

Former Secretary of the Commission on
Marriage and the Home

With the Clinical Help of
ROBERT LATOU DICKINSON, M.D.

Former Secretary of the Committee on Maternal
Health at the Academy of Medicine in New York;
Former President of the American Gynecological Society

HAWTHORN BOOKS, INC.
Publishers / NEW YORK
A Howard & Wyndham Company

Other Books
by LELAND FOSTER WOOD
published by Hawthorn Books, Inc.

BEATITUDES FOR THE FAMILY AND OTHER VERSES
140 meditations in free-verse form
on the true aims and values of Christian family living.

HOW LOVE GROWS IN MARRIAGE
(REVISED EDITION, 1960)
A standard handbook
to help couples make the most of marriage.

HARMONY IN MARRIAGE

Copyright © 1939, 1949, 1955, 1960, 1971 by Round Table Press. Copyright under International and Pan-American Copyright Conventions. All rights reserved, including the right to reproduce this book or portions thereof in any form, except for the inclusion of brief quotations in a review. All inquiries should be addressed to Hawthorn Books, Inc., 260 Madison Avenue, New York, New York 10016. This book was manufactured in the United States of America and published simultaneously in Canada by Prentice-Hall of Canada, Limited, 1870 Birchmount Road, Scarborough, Ontario.

Library of Congress Catalog Card Number: 73–10224.

ISBN: 0-8015-3288-4

REVISED EDITION 1971

7 8 9 10

PRINTED IN THE UNITED STATES OF AMERICA

CONTENTS

iv   Contents

FOREWORD

MARRIAGE IS AN art that calls for the best that we can put into it. The wisest young people are seeking to build their marriages on foundations of good understanding of the physical, mental, social and spiritual factors that make for its success. We say that love is a many-splendored thing, and we want its splendors to grow and never to fade away.

Mature love in marriage leads to mutual enrichment of life, finer comradeship, creative use of differences, with passionate kindness and mutual devotion. So it preserves the values of the romantic love of courtship and adds new and sturdier values of its own. Couples who help their courtship love to grow into the richer maturity of married love will have marriage that is dependable, and that is worth everything to them. Such marriages will also enhance the other fine experiences of life. We want not merely to have marriage that holds together but that is unusually fine and satisfying.

This book is an outgrowth of the author's own happy experience in marriage, of his work as secretary of the Commission on Marriage and the Home and his experience as a counselor for a third of a century. One member of the commission, the late Robert

Latou Dickinson, M.D., most eminent medical authority on marriage, rendered service of the greatest value as a special adviser.

It is a pleasure to acknowledge my indebtedness to publishers who have generously granted permission to quote copyrighted material, to other friends who have helped by criticism, suggestion or encouragement, and especially to Georgia Heaton Wood, my late wife, who shared with me in a lifelong honeymoon, and was an invaluable helper in all my work.

Now that this book has a circulation between a million and two million copies, I am grateful to all who have recommended and distributed it, and to those couples who have reported that they have found help in it. Even to many older couples it has given clues which helped them turn their marriages from failure to success.

LELAND FOSTER WOOD

Chapter I

WHAT MARRIAGE MEANS

ALTHOUGH A WEDDING is a happy and sacred event it is mainly a promise of what is to be. Marriage as a reality in our inner being is not something that can be performed for us, but an achievement which we must work out for ourselves. The marriage vows are loving and lovely, and living them out promotes inner growth and emotional completeness. For the two their marriage will be a creative growth of oneness which can be as fine as they make it. It is their center of gracious living.

CREATING AND SHARING HAPPINESS

A minister can perform the ceremony, and on occasion can give inspiration and guidance of incalculable value, but the real process of unity must be begun, continued and perfected by the two most concerned.The distinction between the wedding and the real marriage was grasped by a young man of limited means who, in speaking of himself and his chosen said that they would not have much of a wedding but a wonderful marriage.

That love has inspired great music, art and literature has often been pointed out. More cheering for most of us is the fact that it is the spring of vitality and of joy in countless lives of everyday people.

As there are many things to learn about marriage and few persons have been educated for this art in any adequate way, the husband and wife may take the attitude of learners, finding out gradually how to live together at their best. As they do this they will experience not only the anticipated joys of home life, but also growing satisfactions and from time to time pleasant surprises.

Since we bring to marriage all that we have and all that we are, and stake our happiness on its success, we should learn to give wholesome expression to all that makes for physical, mental, social and spiritual well-being. In married living the various types of personal needs should be brought to harmonious fulfilment.

When people are resourceful in marriage they learn the art of living at their best. In an atmosphere of love they see new excellences in each other. In the strength of such a relationship the husband and wife have the opportunity of finding their highest happiness together. A person who succeeds in marriage is a success in life though he may fail in many things, while any other success will hardly make up for failure at the very heart of life. As you build up your marriage you build your happiness.

The man and woman entering marriage will ask

such questions as the following: How can we keep love on a high level and at the same time on a practical plane? How can we be at our best in the home? How can we increase each other's more happy moments and decrease the less happy ones? How can we build a shared happiness based on the quality of our life and somewhat independent of outward events and circumstances? How in a world of uncertainty can we find a certainty of love and trust in each other?

The discovery of answers to questions such as these is not easy but answers can be found by almost any couple who will seek them in the right way. And the search has led many to a permanent experience even more rewarding than they had anticipated. Alice Freeman Palmer, who had been dean of women at the University of Chicago, in a letter to a friend wrote about her marriage in these words: "I don't know what will happen if life goes on growing so much better and brighter each year. How does your cup manage to hold so much? Mine is running over, and I keep getting larger cups." * The number of people who find marriage a splendid thing is large enough to encourage us all, yet the secret of most complete comradeship is missed by some really fine people who might have succeeded and still may.

In a venture requiring delicate adjustments, it is necessary that there should be mutual understanding

* George H. Palmer, *The Life of Alice Freeman Palmer*, pp. 211–12, Houghton, Mifflin Co., Boston.

and a common purpose. Is there anything that deserves more careful attention than the success of the home? Other plans may fail without wrecking happiness, but one's marriage is intimately a part of one's self.

While devotion is of the essence of a good marriage, understanding also is needed to keep things at their best. In marriage as in any other great undertaking we must face the question, "Do I understand how to make good in this relationship?"

Success comes when loyalty, wholeheartedness and mutual understanding reinforce one another in a blending of two lives. As musical notes in right combination produce harmony, while the same notes inharmoniously arranged give nothing but discord, so the elements of human nature and personality in the family may be adjusted in pleasing relationships, but if they are not so adjusted, even those persons who might be most happy may make each other miserable. Marriage is truly a duet in this respect and the two performers will have just what they create. If two persons find some discords in the duet of marriage it will not mean that they need to stop the music, but that they need to harmonize their playing, so to meet each other's needs and to build each other's confidence and joy.

The self-centered person tests all things by the question, "Am I getting in marriage the happiness which I deserve?" And yet it is unfair to raise that question without an accompanying one: "Am I giving

in marriage the best that is possible for me to give?"
Two persons thinking of each other's happiness will
find themselves sharing a rich store of durable satisfactions.

An important part of our reward in marriage, as
in life, is gained indirectly. The mature and unselfish
person finds satisfaction in knowing that others receive
joy through him, while the selfish and undeveloped
person thinks mainly of himself and is thus handicapped in marriage.

Two persons who love each other can enrich their
common life by building up a wealth of pleasant as
sociations through good times together, delicate forms
of endearment, little courtesies in the home, shared
enthusiasms, tasks accomplished together, mutual help
in difficulty and a hundred daily experiences of love
and mutual appreciation.

Out of such material each can create a world of
happiness for the other, for the person who receives
daily tokens of appreciation is easier to live with and
the reality that we seek in marriage, as in life, is not
something that we find but something we create.

MARRIED LOVE FULFILLING COURTSHIP LOVE

In marriage a person rightly seeks his own happiness, but even more he dedicates himself to the happiness of the other. The one who most truly brings
joy into the life of the other will most surely have it
for himself. It is easy to think of one's own pleasure.

A child can do that. But it takes a finer growth of personality to be able to devote one's self to the creation of a shared happiness, for happiness is most gained when it is most given. In part the wonderful gift of love comes without our planning. It is something that we fall into, but it is much more than that. It is a life undertaking of two persons who not only feel that their lives will be happier if they are together, but who set out with a determination to make life more satisfactory for each other and to heal each other's hurts.

Toward this end each will consider the needs, wishes and ambitions of the mate, and will learn how best to provide comradeship, help, appreciation, encouragement and whatever else the mate happens most to desire. A happy partner is a test of our success in marriage. Some things please and others annoy. The strategy of harmony is for each to learn how to increase the pleasing experiences and avoid causing annoyance.

In developing all the forms of attraction that two people can have for each other, physical attraction is only one part, although a pleasing one. We can see that God himself intended the sexes to be attractive to each other, but this completely fulfils its purpose only when it is a token of a deeper sharing of life.

Married lovers should develop in mental comradeship also, sharing their thoughts, respecting each other's viewpoints and learning how best to stimulate and supplement each other. Mutual fulfilment and fulness of joy come into a marriage as each brings into it the supplementing and the satisfactions which enrich the life of the other. True marriage is a close comradeship in which each grows in ability to communicate and into deeper understanding of the other's needs. This comradeship becomes a great satisfaction in itself, and has its reward in the avoidance of unnecessary frustrations.

The love of the two is further enriched in happy relationships with family and friends of each other. The husband and wife should realize that each can delight the heart of the other by making a good impression, for it is a joy to a wife if she can feel proud of her husband in the presence of her associates, and to the husband if his wife is highly regarded by his comrades. Marriage is not merely an affair of two in the moonlight, but of two people unified through love in the midst of all the relationships in which they move. Sharing their comradeships will add to the unity of their lives, and will help each to a deeper appreciation of the other.

Spiritual growth also is needed for a complete marriage. This is experienced as the lovers adventure together in the highest life. When people love deeply it gives them an urge to struggle toward the heights, for love has an essential kinship with all that is excellent. Love is of God, and the love of true hearts in wedlock is also of God, making the individual want to be his best for the other and for the home. This means that in marriage we need God's constant help and blessing.

Two persons joined together in marriage will have a measure of agreement, and also, certain differences in their thinking and feeling about spiritual matters. Each should learn to appreciate the ideals of the other, and if either realizes that the other has taken higher ground he should seek to come up to it and share it. At the same time each should take the attitude that life is growth and that there are greater heights above those to which we have attained. Love itself is more satisfying when it is on an upward path.

Love is both material and spiritual, tangible and intangible. We build ourselves into our house of dreams: we grow into our world of happiness; for love is not a fragment of life, or a part of us; it is the whole of us lifted to rapture in our relationships with a special person. While we often regard love as a way of feeling, it is just as much a way of thinking and acting. As feeling, it is a sense of joy in an adored person; as thought, it is understanding and planning for the other; and as action it means all this carried out in behavior. Love is most perfect when it is turned into the art of complete living; quickening the emotions, stimulating our appreciations, giving vigor to our purposes and enlarging our outlook.

Married love is love woven into the fabric and pattern of living. Love is deeper than speech but also it needs to be spoken. It is taken for granted but also it should be constantly renewed and revealed in word and action. Because we love each other the daily experiences of marriage are lifted on a tide that bears us along toward the true goal of living.

RELATIONSHIPS WITH FAMILY, FRIENDS AND COMMUNITY

Not only are the individuals united in marriage, but each becomes in a sense a member of the other's family also, and so each should cultivate the best relationships with the family of the other. The bride or groom should not try to draw the mate too far from his original group, for though married, each needs some of the old loyalties; because memories and associations of the first home are woven into the very fibre of one's being. These, to be sure, now take second place to the new relationship, but they do not fade out of the picture.

While carrying undue emotional dependence upon parents into a person's marriage may be a real danger, it is to be realized also that severing earlier ties too drastically takes something from the joy of life. Fathers, mothers, brothers, sisters and other dear ones still mean much to married persons. As the husband and wife create new domestic foundations for their lives, their ties to their childhood homes will still remain, although in a changed form. We should use these to help the marriage, not to cripple it.

If any of the in-laws are at first unfriendly, the married person should enter upon a campaign of patient good will and acts of friendliness which will in time break down barriers. Some in this way have become finer persons and had better marriages.

It is helpful if husband and wife can enjoy their friendships together. No person will like all members of a mate's social groups equally, but if a husband or wife disapproves of some it is better to speak appreciatively of those who are liked than to criticize those who are not. As far as possible the married person should learn to accept the partner's friendship world and to share his own. At the same time each should recognize the occasional value of some friendships which may not be shared.

Keeping old friends and making new ones will create a circle of cordiality and warmth about the family and will broaden the interests of the home. Old friends of one become new friends of the other, and every well managed marriage enlarges the circle of comradeship. In a growing union of life the two will think not of "your crowd" and "my crowd" but of "our crowd," not "your family and my family," but "our families."

The couple should move in groups which stand for the best things, and should take responsibility for building around themselves the sort of world that is desirable as a setting for homes and an environment for children. The family with a strong circle of friends has firm support for its homemaking endeavor.

Happy is the family
  Whose house is much frequented
By persons of loyalty and worth,
Their strength is a support and stay,
  And they give the wealth of themselves.
Their gifts of mind and spirit
  Lend atmosphere to the home.
And they extend the horizon
  By a new point of view.*

Having paid our tribute to the importance of friends and family connections, let us also recognize that it is desirable for young people to set up a home for themselves whenever possible. A relative is usually better as an occasional visitor than as a member of the household. There are exceptions, of course, but this rule is doubly true of any in-law who would seek to interfere in the affairs of the new home. While the old loyalties are important the new one is supreme, and it is not fair to allow any person, however dear, to "edge in" between husband and wife. Before marriage these two persons were primarily son and daughter in their parental homes, but now they are primarily husband and wife in their own new home. This is a precious kind of independence that should be safeguarded.

The cultivation of supreme loyalty within the home, of neighborliness with other families, of fellowship in church, and of good citizenship in the com-

* The beatitudes used in this book are from *Beatitudes for the Family and Other Verses,* by this author, published by the Round Table Press.

munity gives family life its true significance, provides a set of wholesome relationships for the married pair, and creates a sound basic unit in community living.

PARTNERSHIP IN DAILY WORK

The family is a partnership in domestic business, and each partner should learn to make his finest contribution to the common cause. The married person values the services that are rendered in keeping the home, and in providing for its support, infinitely more because they are services of love.

A good home helps each member to perform his duties more effectively, and this is made still more likely if each shows an interest in the work of the other. A home-minded person does not think of his work as drudgery. Though work is a necessity it is also an expression of personality, and every person who does a common task well improves the world. In the family's vocational life the ordinary motives of skill and of pleasure in accomplishment are reinforced by the knowledge that its work aids the success of other families as well as its own.

Because woman's work in the home can be done by fewer hands than in earlier times, and because of special interests and aptitudes, many women work outside, but if the wife continues with a job, she must not give so much of herself to business that she sacrifices her success at home.

People sometimes overlook the fact that the same

principle applies to a man, and that a husband may become so engrossed in business, profession or some kind of sport, that he gives too little of himself to his home. The ideal is to keep all things in proportion and to set the various departments of life in a harmonious plan in which the details receive attention and the main aims are kept in view.

If a woman is a home-keeper, she may realize that there is nothing the world needs more than good homes. While home-making can be slighted, it may also be made a fine art. Moreover the home is a co-operative workshop of many unseen values and is a producer of artists, educators, public servants and all the other builders of the better world for which we labor.

GROWING TOGETHER

In marriage the individuals have an opportunity to keep on growing, and to improve their adjustments both in the home and in the world outside. As personality is in a constant process of development, for better or for worse, each should set his aim at being the best and most complete person he can become. Especially should one strive to develop in himself those qualities which make one more lovable and those which give flavor to his personality, that each may be an increasingly satisfactory person as a life companion.

The new homemakers have many kinds of abilities

that are worth developing, and each should encourage the other in the development of these abilities in order that family life may be enriched the more. Let the young woman continue her reading, her music, or whatever other artistic or intellectual aspirations she may have; let the husband likewise develop his ability in his chosen line of work and any other talents that he possesses. In this way each will be a strong encouragement to the other, and they will keep up with a fast-moving world.

It is not necessary that the two should have the same education, nor that their interests should be identical, but it is essential that they should supplement and reinforce each other in their world of common thought and understanding. Each can enrich the thinking of the other and add to the insight of the other by being an interesting person to live with. Therefore, each ought to be growing intellectually that there may be a real marriage of minds. They should read together and enjoy good radio and television programs, if possible, and on occasion should attend good plays and lectures together. Each should be big enough to appreciate what the other knows and how the other feels.

An important part of our growth takes place through our interests, because a person's interests are a large part of himself. When any two persons share their enthusiasms they make life more appealing to each other. Such sharing is the very stuff of which marriage is made on the mental side. There is a double reward: we get more out of the shared idea because we enjoy it together, and we create a finer sharing of experience because of the enriching quality of the idea.

Working together in great causes offers a grand opportunity of developing unity because common enthusiasms bind us together and as we share our efforts to create a better world, life grows broader and deeper. People should give their best to each other in mind and thought, not holding back nor fearing that they will give too much, because one who "loses" his smaller self in devotion to the interests of the family will find a larger personality and a richer life.

MAKING MUCH OF HOME LIFE

Because of the many changes which have taken place since the time of our forefathers, when a greater part of the necessary work was done in the home, and as families have given up some of the functions which they used to perform, there are persons who mistakenly suppose that marriage has lost some of the meaning which it used to have.

But the truly essential things in marriage remain, such as the response of heart to heart, the thrill of understanding, sharing joys and sorrows, planning together for children, mutual support in difficulty, loving companionship, and finding a deeper meaning of life in the heart of the other.

Such close relationships are more important now than ever because marriage is on a more distinctly personal basis. While the family has become less necessary as a mere means of production and outward security its place becomes even more vital as a source of deep satisfactions and intangible securities.

In marriage two people achieve a higher completeness of experience, as the narrower "I" feelings grow into richer and more satisfying "we" feelings. So there is at the same time a losing of the smaller self and a gaining of a more complete personality in the common purposes of the family. Marriage is so deep and intimate a relationship that it is sure to affect what a person is to find in life and what kind of person he is to become.

For homemakers the essence of living well together is to make much rather than little of the shared experiences, always giving high regard to the things we do and think and enjoy in common until the very heart of our being is a blending of personalities. Far from being a matter of declining importance, marriage for those who know what they are doing is the most vital thing we have and the quality of it can be enriched almost without limit.

VISTAS

Happy is the pair
  Whose experience is wonder and beauty.
For love opens new vistas,
  And pleasanter paths are found
By two who walk in comradeship,
  Than by one who is alone.

Chapter II

HOW MARRIAGE CAN SUCCEED

A FINE HOME life is an achievement worth planning for as carefully as we plan for any other accomplishment of supreme importance. With reasonable thought and care it is about as easy to learn to live together rightly as to drift into ways of living together wrongly, and it makes all the difference in the world which we do. Let us, then, ask what will help us to keep the satisfying taste in marriage. A good score on the following points will help make marriage what we want it to be.

MAINTAINING PERSONAL ATTRACTIVENESS

That attractiveness which first won the attention and approval of the mate should be guarded and enhanced. After marriage it is no less important than before, for we all like to be happy when we look at those who are dearest to us.

While beauty of personality is of supreme importance and outward appearance is in comparison a secondary matter, yet our impression of any person, even one who is closest to us, comes partly through appearance. That part of personal attractiveness, therefore, which depends upon care and good taste deserves attention. Let the young man be proud to look well for his wife, and the wife meet her husband with something of the care for her appearance and with the gladness of heart which she showed in courtship days. Love is partly admiration and it is desirable to make a good bid for the continued admiration of one's mate.

Still more important than outward care are expressions of the face, for in it kindness, sincerity, and affection are expressed in many subtle ways. If you have these you will look well to your mate. While the physical appearance is worthy of careful attention the attractiveness of a love-revealing countenance with character behind it is beyond computation. A love-revealing face is a beautiful face. Outward attractiveness is a gift of nature but attractiveness of character is an expression of one's self.

If you continually wear for your mate those expressions which come from a true and loving heart, you will be constantly registering agreeably, whereas if you show irritability and unpleasantness, there is little chance for you to be attractive. Each should also make it possible for the face of the other to show pleasure and confidence. How your comrade looks is partly a matter of your own determining—happy or sad, pleased or irritated.

A writer in the field of art has said: "Art is beauty, and beauty is 'from within out,' not 'from without in.' Its quality is eternal. Beauty of mind, if it exist, may express itself unconsciously in whatever one does. Some people with very homely and ordinary features are, when thinking and acting rightly, truly beautiful." *

Almost or quite as important is the habit of making the best use of our voices. When we speak of the cultivation of the voice we usually think of the singer, the public speaker, the actor, the radio, TV or screen artist. But all the joy and inspiration which come into life through such voices are slight compared with the incalculable benefits that follow when people cultivate persistently the art of using pleasant voices at home. A loving voice used with courtesy and consideration is a beautiful voice, and a mingling of such voices rings bells of joy in the heart and gives quality to any home.

HELPING EACH OTHER

When the mates help and strengthen each other they strengthen the home. As the various mechanisms which the family uses, such as a car or refrigerator, run best when all the adjustments are right, and even a good piece of equipment will run badly if it is out of adjustment, so it is with the home itself. Your married life will run more smoothly if the daily program and the habits of each member are adjusted to the other as nearly as possible. Keep similar hours and

* *Interior Decoration: Its Principles and Practice,* by Frank Alvah Parsons, Doubleday Doran, p. 14.

make the moments count. Budget your time so that there will be opportunity for happy hours together. Go out together to well chosen places which both en-joy, and do not forget to cultivate the pleasures of home. Learn to like the same things. When out in company let each aid the other, not competing for at-tention, but helping the other to appear at his best and each being a help-joy, never a kill-joy to the other.

Avoid little inconveniences which hurt because they may give the impression that one does not care. Many unnecessary tensions arise when people thwart and hamper each other. Each should be able to feel that all his interests are more secure because of the other, and that it is easier to live a satisfactory life because of the mate.

The changes of experience bring us now to the need of fulfillment with another, and again to the desire for self-realization as individuals. In marriage there is a fine balancing of freedom and team-play. The individual is free but not too independent; unique, but not separate. No one wants to be a door-mat, yet one must not be so independent that the other cannot get along with him. This results in loneliness and frustration. We find life most fully when we share it, and we find our best selves in each other's hearts. Let each married person give generous scope for the development of the individuality of the other. To hamper the other is to impoverish also the self. Tagore has said:

"Let my love like sunlight, surround you
And yet give you illumined freedom." *

COURTESY AT HOME

Courtesy gives an agreeable tone to the home and makes cooperation pleasant. If people are courteous to friends and strangers, is there any less reason for being so to those who are closest? Not formality, of course, but considerateness in word and action. Countess Clarita de Forceville has well said, "If love is the foundation of happy marriage good manners are the walls and roof." † To use at home words or tones that would be considered uncivil elsewhere is to strike at the foundations.

Husbands and wives are known by the manners they use. This is true not only out in the world but also at home. It is a mark of a gentleman for the husband to show his wife as much courtesy as he could show to any woman. She, of course, will want always to show the high quality he desires in her.

The courteous husband will let his wife go through doorways first, will help her with her rubbers and coat, will pull out her chair, perhaps, and carry her book or package when they are together on the street. Both at home and in company the wife will want to make it

---

* *Fireflies* by R. Tagore, p. 17, by permission of The Macmillan Company, New York, publishers.
† *Marriages Are Made at Home* by Clarita de Forceville, p. 37. Alfred A. Knopf, Inc., New York.

evident that she appreciates his attention, just as she would if they were not yet married. Uniting two lives in courtesy is a help in keeping them united in love.

It is a part of courtesy to be more aware of virtues than of faults. Some persons wear blinders for virtues and use a microscope for faults. Criticisms must be made at times, but they should be made in private and with utmost of consideration for the other as a person. Marriage is more than friendship, but certainly it cannot thrive if it is less. It is a friendship of the most intense and satisfying sort, and like other friendships it needs the touches of exquisite care.

A HELPFUL EMOTIONAL ATMOSPHERE

The home has varieties of emotional tone, as the ocean has varieties of weather. A harmonious family creates its own sunshine and a stormy one makes its own tempests. Emotional strain is sometimes occasioned by mere thoughtlessness which proves more irritating than the guilty member realizes. Joy or bitterness is largely an outcome of the cultivation and guidance of the emotions. While this applies to all personal relationships, it is especially weighty in marriage. Emotional attitudes may be either the positive and constructive emotions of love and trust, or the negative and potentially destructive emotions of fear, hatred and resentment. Every expression of love strengthens the bonds of the home, creating happy memories and increasing the pleasure tone of family experience, while outbursts of anger, peevishness or bitterness harm the unity which marriage aims to set up.

The score of family success is raised by acts of delicate mutual consideration, and lowered by every outburst of irritation. Anger, however, is not a sign that the marriage has failed. Occasional outbursts may be met constructively if the persons will penetrate beyond the mere upheaval and face the unsolved problem or unrelieved tension which caused the flare-up.

Much possible unhappiness can be prevented if each will take pains to realize how the other feels. The same person can be pleasing at some times and irritating at others, and the one who is inclined to be careless can correct these tendencies and get in the habit of giving pleasure and avoiding things that annoy the other.

Each member can determine his own behavior and in part that of the other. If we are loving we are likely to have love in return, but if we show harsh and critical attitudes we are almost certain to provoke resentment and opposition so we get what we ask for. Angry outbursts tend to produce angry responses. When, however, irritability is simply due to fatigue or ill health it should be soothed at the surface and treated at its source.

Gentle words calm tense situations, but harsh words cut like whips. An old rule is to count ten when angry before speaking, another is for both not to be angry at the same time. Recognize that anger is a signal that something needs correcting, probably as much in the disposition of the one who is angry as in the behavior of the other. It is easy to say too much when angry. Anybody can do that. But it is a fine achievement to analyze the situation in which anger arose and to find some constructive solution. When people who are otherwise lovable fail to restrain their tempers their words should not be taken too seriously. On the other hand, the person who has said an unkind thing ought to make amends. This is a debt which every self-respecting person should pay, and the one to whom it is due should receive it with affectionate response, not as a thing demanded. A difficulty overcome can be a stepping stone to better things.

One test of a good home is its ability to heal little hurts and forget many things that would cause irritation. If these are put behind our backs, they are harmless, but if piled up between us, small bits of unpleasantness finally produce a wall of separation. For this reason little misunderstandings ought to be cleared up as soon as possible, and the two ought to have the rule never to begin or close the day with any hurts unhealed or offenses unforgiven. Let the harmony of the home be like a tapestry which either member would hate to tear. If torn it may be mended, but it is better not torn.

There is no doubt that much trouble is caused when people in a nervous or critical attitude make mountains out of molehills and create tempests over trifles which could be turned aside with tact and a sense of humor. To laugh over difficulties often cuts them down to size. We naturally do this when things are going well, and even when difficulties or misfortunes must be met two people who love each other can still laugh because they have their greatest happiness in each other.

Confidence and mutual trust build up happiness while fear and anxiety tend to drive it away. While some forms of fear and anxiety have to do with circumstances over which we have little control, yet it can make a world of difference whether we center our attention on the hopeful and constructive features of a situation or on those elements in it which are dark and discouraging.

There is no situation so favorable that a gloomy aspect may not be thrown over it by conjuring up all possible grounds of anxiety, and there is none so unfavorable as to be without some ray of hope. Hope is the child of a vigorous imagination seeing possible ways out of difficulty and new pathways toward success. Two people with hopeful spirit can find real happiness even in the midst of difficult circumstances, and with such an attitude they are in a better position to improve their circumstances.

If you are married to a person who suffers from

anxieties and fears, be sympathetic but do not fall into his moods of gloom, rather let your attitude of courage and good cheer brighten the atmosphere. Take these emotional fears and worries in a scientific spirit; make them unnecessary so far as possible, and help your partner to overcome them by thinking thoughts of happiness and confidence. At the same time realize that a person's moods are not to be changed by mere exhortation and that underlying problems can best be discussed when the mate is in a more cheerful frame of mind.

One of the most necessary forms of confidence is confidence in ourselves. The home provides a service of greatest value when it gives the individual a place where his necessary self-esteem receives support. By building such a home two people provide a refuge from the storms which beat inevitably upon every life. Whatever stress individuals have to bear outside, whether of opposition, conflict, disapproval or misunderstanding, those tensions should be relieved in their own home. For this reason each member ought to be sensitive to the strains that the other has to bear and ingenious in providing a refuge. In the quiet haven of mutual confidence troubles can be forgotten, or at least cut down to size. That is one reason why they should not be hashed over more than necessary.

The world wounds us at times, let the home heal us. The world deflates personality, let the home restore it. It is of inestimable value to a person if he can have a place where he is first, and where all that concerns him is of supreme interest to another. If, however, in addition to normal strain and stress outside there is tension at home, where it affects us most deeply, we make each other unhappy and may even wreck a good marriage.

The husband tired from his duties deserves to come to a home of rest and comfort; and the wife who has struggled during the day, whether at home or out in the world, should find quietness of heart at evening time, either in her home or in pleasing social contacts in company with a husband who understands her needs. Many a person goes out to win his battles through the constant help and reinforcement of his home, and such a one has a strength and poise hard to beat down. Let both work together to make their home a tower of strength and a citadel of peace.

The most important of all causes of emotional security or insecurity, of confidence or fear, are usually within the close relationships of the mates themselves. No external circumstances can give such full assurance as the complete trust of the two in each other, and no outside occurrence can strike one down so completely as a blow from within, caused by any cruelty or disloyalty.

Artistry in family living is a matter of the skilful cultivation of love and confidence and eliminating or at least making constructive use of any angers or fears that arise. Careless drifting in turbulent waters may lead to shipwreck. Every situation which tends to call out anger or fear should be re-examined and reconstituted in such a way that love and trust will take over again. Even when outward conditions are discouraging, love and confidence will bind two people together in such a way that they can carry on more successfully.

Jealousy is a combination of emotional insecurity with anger and resentment at some real or fancied attack upon the integrity of love. It sometimes arises from thinking of one's own need of love while the other's need of it is overlooked. If jealousy arises it may be unfounded and yet difficult to deal with. It is an occasion for thinking much but speaking little. Often it is as much a sign that the marriage needs attention from within as that it is attacked from without. To meet the situation constructively by giving renewed love is better than to indulge in suspicions or upbraidings. Jealousy sometimes arises because one of the pair is too possessive or too suspicious, making much of little matters which might better be ignored.

If you are jealous it means that you are not quite sure you are making your love satisfying to your mate. Then if you deal with the situation by a scene or a curtain-lecture, you make the wound deeper and run the risk of alienating the other, perhaps unjustly. It is better to deal with it by drawing so close together that it will be hard for anything to come between you. As you do not wish to suffer the pangs of jealousy in your own heart, be even more careful not to give occasion for it in the heart of your mate.

Emotional difficulties are danger points. They may arise out of some immaturity in personal development or they may be due to some sort of situation which these two have not yet learned to handle. In most cases they are best met by building up a large fund of understanding, of confidence and of common interests. As little physical symptoms often disappear when radiant health is gained, so also many emotional symptoms vanish like shadows when love shines with steady light and there are real goals ahead.

GOOD TIMES TOGETHER

It adds to the joy of marriage if each person cultivates the arts of being interesting, amusing and encouraging, and also of being a good listener, appreciative of what the other says and does. One needs to learn to enjoy the good traits of the person to whom one is married and even to appreciate on occasion his amiable imperfections.

Homes that are gay with laugher and good cheer bear the burdens of life more easily, and blows of difficulty and adversity do not destroy them. Fun and laughter lighten burdens of fatigue and care, and at the same time promote harmony and give life a good taste. Recreation is well named when it recreates, and every home ought to build into its experience plenty of good times planned and carried out together. Therefore, the two should be alert to find and take advantage of the available things that are fun to do together.

While men have their sports and games and women have their special interests, there is a large place for happy times in which the husband and wife play together. If the husband likes hiking, camping, boating and swimming, let not the wife be content to live merely an indoor life. If the wife enjoys concerts, plays and social gatherings, the husband may well learn to share these pleasures if he does not already value them. Each wants to give the other a full and glowing life, and each may gain, even from the personal point of view, by learning to enjoy the things the other likes.

> Happy is the wife
>   Who knows how to be a playmate
> To share and enrich her husband's leisure
>
> And happy the husband,
>   Who is a giver of good times,
> And a comrade to his wife.
>
> For many burdens and cares
>   Must be shared within the home,
> But in good times together,
>   They lay up larger stores of joy.

CONTINUING TO BE LOVERS

The vows at the altar do not make further courtship unnecessary, but prepare the way for it to be more complete. Persons who have learned how to please each other before marriage ought to continue to develop this art afterwards. Law, custom and a marriage certificate cannot make a home, and even the promise to love while life shall last is not enough unless it is carried out continually in words and acts. Married people should be lovers and sweethearts no less than engaged people are, but more, each stimulating the normal love impulses of the other by being easy to love. The period before marriage is an apprenticeship in love. After marriage comes the greater and growing fulfillment.

People who continue their lovemaking at home do not need to seek comfort from outside adventures, nor even to spend much on expensive entertainment; but the home in which either one is starved in the emotional expression of love is a disappointing one and more subject to the invasion of outside attachments.

Emotional non-support may be as serious as financial non-support in its effect on the inner life of the pair. Do not take everything for granted, but make your love so secure that if the choice of life partners were to be made over again each would choose the other. Remember that your mate has a perfectly natural desire for attention and appreciation from you.

Be certain that you measure up to the pattern of affection to which your mate has been accustomed. If the bride's father was an ideal lover to her mother do not be less so to her. If the bridegroom's mother set a high ideal of affection and tenderness, do not fall short of that standard. If, on the other hand, the childhood home was less than happy there is all the more reason for going to the opposite extreme so completely as to stamp out any fear that unhappiness may be normal in married life. In giving affection do not be surpassed by any other home.

Many forms of skill in being one's best and in bringing out the best in the other express a will to succeed in life's finest adventure, and a shared will to succeed keeps us on the crest of a wave moving toward fulfillment.

Chapter III

HOW CAN MONEY HELP
OR HINDER?

How WE USE money helps or hinders the success of marriage. Many families make this side of their life a real expression of mutual regard and team-work. Some have difficulties caused by outside factors over which they have little control, but are like good sailors taking the waves with skill. Careful planning is needed. In some families immature spending habits lead to trouble, in others troubles over money are symtoms of disharmonies of purpose and personality that lurk beneath the surface and the partners quarrel about money because that is easy to talk about. Couples who find themselves bickering about money should ask themselves whether this is what they are truly unhappy about: it is more helpful to face the real issues honestly than to wound and bruise each other over a false issue which could be resolved with good sense and loving cooperation.

CHOOSING OUR GOALS

In a practical way the family must study how to meet its needs wisely, to live within its income, to avoid unnecessary debt, to provide for security and to plan for advancement.

One of the easiest roads to trouble is the effort to make an impression. Among all forms of freedom one of the most helpful is freedom from the notion that if the Joneses are extravagant we must keep pace with them. Actually they are probably being run ragged trying to keep up with us. Emancipation from such folly is a part of growing up and is necessary to peace and harmony People must have the courage to live their own lives.

The scale of living is not an end in itself, yet some families needlessly sacrifice peace of mind to a misguided struggle for wealth, thus becoming so busy, so burdened and so anxious that there is little room in their lives for love and fellowship. Thus they make themselves poor by sacrificing the greater values for the lesser ones. Many a couple in the wisdom of being grateful for what they have rather than bitter about what they lack, work their way up together and meet hardships skilfully. A pair who later became famous said that there were times during the first five years of their marriage when neither of them could mail a letter because they did not have enough to buy a stamp. But they had a wonderful time. Poverty is not the greatest handicap, and riches are not in themselves a boon. It is necessary that the material needs be met, but an even greater need is to recognize that material things in the family must be used as aids and means to a more complete life. The home is a setting for love and fellowship, and people who have these things get a good return for their efforts, while lacking these their money is poorly spent however much they have.

In the first place, there must be team-work. Before marriage each made final decisions about spending the personal income, but if one should continue this attitude into marriage he would be carrying a single person's type of mind into a married person's situation. Marriage is a partnership in which each must be considered. Otherwise the partners are not likely to have harmony, for if they put themselves in competition for the income there will never be enough, and this attitude will set them in opposition to each other.

One sees families in which a husband buys luxuries for himself, while not providing spending money for his wife; or he keeps the money in his own hands and doles out small sums, as to a child. A man who spends money freely for himself, but is niggardly toward his wife and never gives her flowers or other tokens of affection is far from being an artist in the use of money; and one who is a despot in financial matters will find it harder to rule over the heart of a mate. If, on the other hand, the wife has brought money into the family she should guard against any tendency to be the boss financially. A wife should face the duties and necessary economies of the home with loving care and thoughtfulness. If she is negligent of the home and uses money carelessly, financial trouble will not be far off. The happiness of a family can be wrecked on such reefs.

Many homemakers have been justly proud of their success in using limited resources with such skill as to achieve a standard of living which usually goes with a higher income. The real level of living, however, is mainly an inner matter: not what the lamps cost, but what kind of books we read in their light; not how elegant the chairs, but what kind of talk we have as we sit in them; not the tableware, but the happy meals together. Even a couple having a hard time financially can have a home which is a treasury of kindness and a citadel of comradeship.

WHEN BOTH WORK OUTSIDE

In many families it is a practical necessity for the wife to work outside as well as the husband, and when this is necessary it should be freely accepted. Freedom of women to work for wage or salary has advantages. In some cases it relieves the necessity of undue postponement of marriage. In others, special abilities of the wife make it desirable for her to work outside the home. Yet marriage itself is the finest sort of a career, and it is detrimental to family life when those women who should be devoting their best talents and energies to the high profession of being wives, mothers and homemakers are compelled to give so much of themselves to the outside world that they have only margins of time to give to their homes. The wife working efficiently at home is a real producer, in some cases saving as much as she would earn elsewhere.

When the wife has a job more help will be needed at home. As the two are both working away from the home during the day it will be all the more fun doing things together in the evening. In those occasional cases in which the wife's earnings are larger that those of the husband, this fact should not cause him undue embarrassment so long as he is doing useful work and doing it well, and especially if he is striving to improve himself in his work. The wage received is not necessarily a gauge of personal worth.

THE BUDGET: A PLAN FOR SPENDING

Most families will have to get into the habit of thinking carefully about their purchases, asking such questions as: Do we need this? Does it fit into our scheme of living? Or will the purchase of this throw our spending out of balance and make it impossible to have things which we need even more?

Such questions will call for a plan of spending, a budget to show where money goes and how far it will reach. Such a plan is a help in buying wisely and keeping out of debt. Some insurance companies and banks have budget books and pamphlets showing how a family should use its income and how its members may make economies without sacrificing well-being. These are well worth having, but any ready-made scheme must be adapted to the particular case.

In a general plan, distinguish between needs and mere wants, and take care of needs first. Make allowance for the type of income; whether a fixed amount, or the fluctuating returns of many occupations. Where the amount per month varies, budgeting will be more difficult, and expenditures should be on a scale allowing for possible shrinkage. There should also be some provision for expenses that no one can foresee, a rainy day fund.

When both are earning it is well to try to live entirely within the husband's income, because the wife's earnings may be interrupted by the coming of children, at which times there will also be extra expenses. It is better if possible to put the wife's earnings into a fund for children and their education, or for the purchase of a home, or for saving. If the family starts out on a budget absorbing the earnings of both, they may have to lower their standard at a time when it will be difficult. Remember that the total income is to be used over a period of years for the greatest good of the family, including children.

Debt is an added load, easy to incur and hard to repay. Beware of borrowing, and do not assume obligations that are likely to strain the family.

A couple may think of their needs under the following headings: Housing; Furniture and Equipment; Food; Clothing; Running Expenses; Health; Improvement; Savings.

Housing. Housing should be chosen for comfort and adaptability to the family's needs. The rent should not be more than one-fourth of the total budget; however, where rents are abnormally high it may be impossible to stay within this limit.

If a house is purchased or built, it should not ordinarily cost more than the income for two and a half years, for it is not wise for any family to load itself with a burden of debt which may enslave them to interest and other payments. Whether the house is owned or rented, care should be used in keeping it in as good condition as possible.

The outward things of the home should minister to the inner values. Restful furniture, ample light, and a well chosen color scheme provide a good start. Add loving looks and zestful cooperation, thus harmonizing outward and inward things.

We get our home values not from the way things look outwardly but from the way we feel inwardly. A man does not want to have things too painfully in place, nor would a child want to have his home so unruffled that he could never play in it, nor have a pillow fight with his parents. The house exists for the family, not the family for the house; therefore, it should be a help and not a burden. It should be supremely a place of fellowship, and a setting for love.

There are satisfactions in owning a home, but also risks. The city family on a small income should consider whether the work situation is dependable or whether there is a likelihood of transfer to some other place. It is to be hoped that greater economic security for all families may become possible so that those families which desire homes of their own may have them.

Furniture and Equipment. Some couples overload themselves by purchasing a houseful of furniture on credit and then, in times of stress, have to give up the furniture and lose all they have paid on it. It is better to begin simply, if necessary, and to buy a few articles at a time, looking around for pieces which can be bought at little expense. Sometimes good furniture has been stored away, so that occasionally a real find may be brought out and refinished for the new home. This is fun and at the same time it rescues some fine pieces from oblivion and puts them to good use. Sometimes excellent pieces may be bought at auctions or at thrift stores at great savings.

When the family buys furniture or equipment it should be guided by its needs rather than by sales pressure. In stores it is better to buy from reliable ones, because there are many things which look good but really are not.

One's home is primarily a place to live in and

not for show. There is little comfort in having costly things if there are worries attached to them. On the other hand, those who have money to spend may well use some of it in beautifying their homes. The reading of one or two good books on interior decoration may make an almost unbelievable difference and, at the same time, involve little extra expense.

Food. Almost any family, with care in buying and preparation of food, may be well nourished on a fraction of what thoughtless spenders use. Both as a homemaker and a hostess the woman who can prepare tasty dishes is prized. Though many young women marry without much experience, the bride should not remain inefficient in these matters. She can study the art of preparing simple and favorite dishes unusually well and serving them in an atmosphere of good cheer, for such meals prepared at home provide a foundation for health as well as a substantial saving. To assure the latter, however, the family must avoid waste. The housewife who wishes to buy most wisely may get the government reports on diet and health.*

The family of limited means should keep away from the expensive places and avoid extravagant entertaining. They should know that fruits, vegetables and fish are cheaper and also better when they are in season, and that it is worth while to find out which

* These can be secured from the U. S. Bureau of Home Economics, Washington, D. C. Free pamphlets issued by the Metropolitan Life Insurance Company of New York also give good advice.

meats are the best buys at any particular time. This will make food dollars go much farther.

Clothing.   Care in buying clothing and keeping it in condition will enable the family to look well on a moderate expenditure, while with carelessness they are not likely to look well on any amount. "A stitch in time saves nine," and the nine are not only laborious but costly. The habit of folding, brushing and hanging up clothing and of keeping shoes in good condition will result in saving, because the wearing apparel will look well as long as it lasts and will not need to be replaced so quickly. True style is a matter of dressing carefully in a way that fits one's individuality rather than being dominated by mere caprice of fashion. A good appearance is a matter of knowledge and study issuing in good taste.

Running Expenses.   Running expenses include such things as heat, light, gas and service. In a well managed household, electricity, gas and water are not wasted, and the heating plant is regulated properly. Little savings in these matters are worthy of attention, for running expenses will run away with the budget if not watched. When necessary, outside service can be dispensed with almost entirely, for it is better to do one's own work than to run into debt to pay others to do it.

Health.   The best medicines are air, water and sunshine, and the best safeguard of health is exercise. For many this comes naturally with work. Others, whose daily program is a sedentary one, should plan carefully for good times together which will also give exercise. Games, hikes, swimming, tennis, shuffleboard and such things are more fun than high priced recreation, and at the same time they are wonderful for health. As hours of work are lessened more time is left for family fellowship.

In addition to the health benefits provided by nature every family will need the care of the family doctor and of the dentist on occasion. Choose these carefully. Regular visits to the dentist give better results and cost less than neglect of the teeth. Prevention is better than cure. Also the family should investigate the group plans for hospital and medical service on the basis of small regular payments, such as the Blue Cross and Blue Shield plans.

There are a number of "don'ts" in the health world. Don't get the habit of depending on the drug store for health. Most of the money spent on patent medicines is wasted. Don't waste money on quacks. Let physical, mental and spiritual health be a by-product of happy, wholesome living.

Health and happiness can be jeopardized by drugs and alcohol. In recent years there has been a striking increase of uninsurability of men under thirty due to alcoholic addiction. A person who for this cause is not insurable is less likely to be a success as a marriage partner. Alcohol has ruined countless homes. Shakespeare commented on the fact that men will "put an enemy in their mouths to steal away their brains." * Cigarettes harm precious lungs, affect the unborn, hasten many deaths and cost good money. People who feel that they simply must follow any custom which others set or advertisers urge will need to get down to more basic thinking if they are to make the most of their lives.

Improvement. Improvement as an item in the budget means that the family needs to spend money for books, magazines, music, recreation, and vacations, as well as for education of children. Under this heading also come the support of the church and charities. A certain broadening of interests results from giving even a little. Whether the income is large or small it is imperative to study how it can be used to gain the greatest amount of real benefit, and to consider how the use of money can promote the greater satisfactions that wealth cannot buy. Contact with great causes opens up new areas of the finest fellowship, educates the family in sympathy and increases its grasp of world affairs.

Saving. The husband and wife ought to plan for saving. It has been found that families which save some of their income make a greater success of their family life. It adds stability as well as convenience to have a bank account. Every family needs the protection of life insurance. The face value of the in-

* *Othello* III, 3, 293.

surance carried should be about twice the annual income for the protection of the wife, and as much again for each child. Premiums should be paid on an annual, or quarterly basis, since weekly payments are much more expensive in proportion. Saving and insurance add to family stability. Small savings added together can become substantial. When these are to be invested beware of get-rich-quick schemes; get the advice of your banker.

A plan for saving will be possible for the ordinary couple only when they guard against loading the financial canoe with a mass of things bought on "easy payments." Sometimes, without reckoning carefully the sum of them, young people assume more obligations than they can carry. To live within one's income is a satisfaction: to live beyond it endangers not only credit but also the rock foundation of personal freedom. Moreover, saving and paying cash for things which we really need makes possible a considerable increase in the number of real needs that we can satisfy. Installment buying is usually expensive business, and buying things that have no real value for us is sheer folly.

OVERCOMING INSECURITY

The breadwinner should have a job that fits him, and should protect it by doing it as well as it can be done. In an age of automation old jobs may disappear, but new ones open for those who are ready. Continued study often pays off well, for yesterday's skills may be inadequate for tomorrow's jobs.

We want a suitable income for our family and all others. The lack of a living wage handicaps home-making efforts and makes it harder for some to take their place in community life. In a time of world turmoil every well-managed home counts on the side of security and peace while homes deprived of economic security or failing to achieve it through their own carelessness add to the forces of unrest.

Every Christian is a member of a brotherhood upon whom the commandment is laid to help one another as we would be helped. Let the homebuilder be also a civilization-builder by contributing to a neighborly and Christian way of life, so that no one will want too much and no family need be in want.

Some booklets and pamphlets for further study—"Money and Your Marriage" by Carl F. Hawver, Roy A. Burkhart and James Peterson, National Consumer Finance Association, Washington, D. C. "How To Avoid Financial Troubles," by Kenneth C. Masteller, American Institute for Economic Research, Great Barrington, Mass. "Mind Your Money," (a) When You Spend, (b) When You Shop, (c) When You Use Credit. Free pamphlets. Household Finance Corp., Prudential Plaza, Chicago, Ill. Others may be had from banks and insurance companies.

Chapter IV

PHYSICAL HARMONY

PEOPLE WHO HAVE a wholehearted and unselfish devotion to each other will learn some things almost instinctively. In some they will need instruction. No person is born a husband or a wife, but the whole-hearted lover can learn to be one or the other. The two must continue to be lovers if they are to know fully what it means to be husband and wife, to love with heart and mind and soul and also to love with the physical nature.

THE POINT OF VIEW

Physical differences enable the mates to benefit and supplement each other in many ways. Marriage is based on them. Without them life would be shorn of the romance of courtship, and the joys of family experience. Because of them, married lovers are able to charm and delight each other in many endearments of daily life.

Differences in emotional response require under-standing. The comparatively steady nature of the husband's emotional life makes it all the more necessary that he understand the ebb and flow of his wife's vitality, from the periods when she is less vigorous physically but unusually sensitive emotionally, to the times when superlatively full of life she longs for fullest renewal of romance. The wife should not expect her husband to share her moods fully, but taking him as he is, she should be delicately skilful in stimulating and accepting his manly impulses of love. With such an understanding the mates will be partners of the closest and dearest kind, and more. The something more is expressed in the sex relationship.

Sex in marriage is not merely a physical experience but an expression of pleasure in marriage itself. However it is not, as some have seemed to think, the only key to marital happiness.* Marriage is a union of personalities and the sex relationship is an expression and a symbol of that union. Harmony in personal relations helps prepare a husband and wife for physical harmony, and vice versa.

Formerly some held that only men were strongly sexed. Now we know that while individuals differ the sexual needs of women are as real as those of men although different. The fact that the sex impulse is more easily aroused in men, and that in some cases it is never fully awakened in women, has misled many about woman's nature, but the wife who is sexually responsive to her husband may congratulate

* Cf. *Psychological Factors in Marital Happiness*, by Lewis M. Terman, McGraw-Hill, p. 376.

herself that she is not lacking in one of the endowments of complete wifehood. She can the more perfectly give and receive full happiness in marriage and can experience a harmony with her husband that will strengthen their union.

The powerful natural energy of sex becomes an aid in marriage when both mates maintain their attractiveness for each other, and when they understand how to use their marital union as an expression of love and of delight in each other.

A helpful point of view about the sexes is given in the Book of Genesis, which says that God made the race male and female. "And God saw every thing that he had made, and, behold, it was very good." *
A contrary idea, coming down from ancient times, is that the body is evil and is an impediment to the soul. This leads to an unnatural view of bodily functions, whereas respect for marriage makes it natural for us to think of marital union as an expression of love and fellowship.

This is in accord with a right understanding of the place of physical things, for they get their meaning in relation to their use. As in the piano the metal and wood, though material, are aids to the production of music, as the fingers of the artist are identified with his work, so the body is an instrument of personality, and not an impediment unless misused.

In marriage the element of mutual respect and of

* Genesis 1:31.

regard for the sacredness of the family makes sexual union a fine and delicate means of expression of the grace of true love. When this expression is frustrated the excellence of the personal relationship is likely to be impaired through resulting nervous tensions. Sexual union in marriage, then, is not thought of as a duty which one mate owes to the other, but as a most intense expression of devotion, in which, as the Bible says, "They shall be one." * So each should value the sexuality of the other.

This also is a reason why sex outside marriage defeats the aim of our complete nature, which calls not merely for an appeasement of the sex hunger, but for a satisfying and stable family life. This gift when used for love and the family builds up personality, but used irresponsibly it makes for a shallow and distorted nature, which cannot permanently satisfy the love needs of marriage. The sexual union of a husband and wife ought to be a symbol and expression of their complete love, trust and self-giving to each other.

SEX DIFFERENCES UNDERSTOOD

A young woman said to an older friend, "I am going to be married, but I don't know what it is all about." There are many like her, and others who know certain things in a misleading way. Persons approaching marriage and others who have entered it

* *Ephesians* 5:31.

ignorantly are likely to need plain and concrete instruction dealing with the functions of the most important organs of sex.

The body is a wonderful creation, and not least so in the organs of sex. Nature provides that the husband's organ for sexual union, the penis, becomes stiff and "erect" for the experience of intercourse, projecting outward at an angle which facilitates entrance into the vagina which is able perfectly to receive it to the mutual pleasure of the mates. At the end of the penis the glans, or head, always maintains a soft and velvety condition favorable for contact. The husband's sexual feeling is largely centralized in the glans. The scrotum, or flexible sac hanging back of the penis, contains the two testicles, which are egg-shaped glands containing a marvelous series of tiny tubules in which sperm cells called spermatozoa are produced for the carrying of life.

In the intermediate structures is manufactured the chemical product called the male sex hormone which circulating day by day in the blood stream beginning at puberty acts to produce the traits of manhood, to aid physical and mental vigor, and to condition the system for sexual sensitivity.

The spermatozoa, which are microscopic in size, exist by hundreds of millions in the semen, a fluid which is produced in the testicles, prostate gland and seminal vesicles, and is discharged at the climax of intercourse. Two small glandular sacs located back of the husband's bladder are called the seminal vesicles. These secrete an opalescent fluid, which with the addition of the secretion of the prostate gland, constitutes a large part of the semen, and acts as vehicle and stimulant for the spermatozoa. These tiny sperm cells are vigorously active in the semen and in the secretions of the vagina, and if one meets and unites with an ovum, or egg, in the body of the wife, conception takes place. Within a minute or two from the time of its discharge the sperm cell may have passed from the vagina into the uterus, and in an hour, or a few hours, it may have reached the oviduct.

As all the sex glands are secreting steadily, the supply of semen and its vehicles at times becomes such that distention occurs all along the tract. This produces a condition of sexual excitability, but nature provides for occasional relief through emission of semen in sleep with sex feeling and usually with an erotic dream. In the case of a married man this distended condition gives an impulse toward the marital relationship with the wife. This urge is therefore a sign of health and love, and should be accepted as such. Since men have known seminal emission from puberty onward the sex urge is more definite in the normal experience of the groom than in that of the virgin bride.

The female sex organs are chiefly internal. Between the thighs lies the vulva with the "outer lips," or fleshy folds, called "labia majora," and the "inner lips," thinner folds, called "labia minora." Beneath the anterior junction of the "inner lips" is a very important organ called the clitoris, whose only purpose is to give sex feeling. This is a sort of miniature female replica of the male organ, and, like the penis, is capable of erection in sex excitement. It is, however, very small. This organ is intensely stimulated by contact and by friction and is the chief center of sexual responsiveness, although there are other parts of a wife's body where she is especially sensitive to loving contact and caressing. The sensitive nerves of sexual responsiveness help prepare her whole body and emotions for the sexual embrace. Therefore a husband should know by experimentation where the sensitive areas are and how to touch, kiss or fondle them to the wife's greatest pleasure.

Within the vulva is the opening of the vagina, a passage lined with mucous membrane and circled by a loop of muscles, which in time of sex excitement relax to contain the husband's organ, and adjust themselves to it perfectly. The inner vulva is provided with glands which secrete a transparent fluid for the purpose of lubrication enabling the husband easily to effect an entrance. However, if the wife's sexual feelings are not aroused the entrance may be dry and unready. In this condition intercourse is likely to give discomfort which defeats the true aim of harmony and mutual delight.

The muscles looped around the vagina are capable also of spasm or closure in some cases of fear and mental antagonism, so that extra gentleness is required to overcome all fear; otherwise the sex relationship may become difficult and unpleasant.

In the condition of virginity the entrance to the vagina is partly covered by a membrane called the hymen, and has an opening that can stretch easily an inch in diameter. Occasionally this opening will have been enlarged by local treatment by a physician. If this membrane remains and is slightly torn by pressure in intercourse, some pain may be experienced in the first act of union.

In the past the few drops of blood thus released have been valued as proof of virginity. However, a woman's virginity may be assured without this particular test. If the bride is willing to have the sex life start with some discomfort or pain, and will make allowances in her mind for this sort of initiation, there is no great difficulty for the majority of women; for in many cases the distress is slight and the bleeding confined to a drop or two, so that even at the start pleasurable feeling predominates.

In a few women, however, the hymen is so thick that treatment is needed. A physician can easily correct the situation in such rare cases. As gentle stretching is one method it is becoming not uncommon for medical counselors to advise self-stretching of the hymen and to let the sensible bride herself undertake the process by dilating the entrance to the vagina daily with her fingers prior to marriage, and, if after marriage there is difficulty, to continue the process. This will usually remedy those cases which would otherwise cause difficulty in early sexual adjustment.

Examination of both parties by a physician is desirable in a number of ways. The doctor's counsel will help the couple meet any special problems they may have, and to remove fears or false ideas.*

At the end of the vagina and at right angles with it is the uterus or womb, which though only three inches long can expand to hold a child. The sperm must pass from the vagina through a narrow neck into the womb if pregnancy is to take place, and in this process some may remain alive and active for as much as forty-eight hours. From the upper and outer corners of the uterus the Fallopian tubes lead right and left to the ovaries.

From the ovaries eggs, one about every twenty-eight days, are released into the Fallopian tubes and into the uterus. The egg may remain alive and fertile for as much as forty-eight hours. If in this time impregnation does not take place the egg, which is the

* If there is any possibility that either may have been infected with venereal disease prompt and thorough treatment by a reputable physician is an absolute necessity, and marriage must be postponed until cure so that infection of the partner is impossible.

size of the tiniest period in print, is expelled and menstruation occurs. The ovaries also produce hormones, which enter the blood stream and produce the traits of femininity.

In physical union it is desirable that the various sex parts should be brought into activity and vitality, each in its appropriate way. Perfect success at the beginning is almost too much to expect, but patience of each with the self and with the other will usually win its reward, for both husband and wife will improve with experience.

THE HONEYMOON

The honeymoon is a time set apart for the beginning of new adjustments, and it ought to be a comparatively brief period free from hurry and distraction. It is better to spend it at some restful place, such as a hotel or cabin by a lake than in traveling and sightseeing. Weddings should be early enough in the day to enable the bride and groom to have their evening together at the first place of destination, rather than to spend it in traveling.

This period may be made a time to which the mates will look back with wonder and delight, and for this reason it is of the utmost importance that the husband and wife should know how to bind their lives together. During these early days it is possible for the husband to show his bride that love in marriage is even more beautiful than anything she has ever known before, and it is worth much if they can start their life together in that way.

Whatever else a wife wants in her husband, the normal wife is sure to want him to be a lover. This will help him during the honeymoon to dissolve any barriers of uncertainty or fear that the bride may have. If, however, he breaks through these barriers too clumsily, the two may remember the beginning of their marriage with unnecessary pain and regret. The husband should not think that just because the wedding has taken place he may demand intercourse, for to approach this experience merely as a right which he can claim may spoil it temporarily for both.

At all times, and especially at the time of timidity and uncertainty of the inception of the new relationship, the wife wants to be courted and loved rather than forced either physically or mentally. Her nature is such that love means everything to her, and the tenderest and most intimate physical expression of union may be made such as to thrill her whole being.

Great gentleness along with strength on the bridegroom's part will be well repaid. As he has wooed her and won her to marriage, all the more should he woo his bride to the new experiences. It is only the occasional woman who will respond best to the caveman type. The bridegroom's purpose is not to grasp something for which he has waited, but to lay a foundation for a lifetime of happiness together.

On the other hand, the bride should not hurt the

husband by regarding his passion as something un-
worthy. This is an affront to his manhood and un-
worthy of her as a complete wife because absence of
response is a limitation on her part.

LOVE PLAY

It is more in accord with the artistry of marriage
to prepare for sexual union in an atmosphere of play
and wooing. In marriage there is not only joy but
playfulness. The husband naturally delights in fon-
dling and caressing his wife, using hands and lips
tenderly and when she is awakened she will want to
respond, each feeling that every part of the body of
the other is inexpressibly precious. Both may enter
into this love play without the slightest fear and with
mutual joy in contacts which give special delight.
Each may well show appreciation to the other.

SEXUAL UNION

When the husband is able to make his wife feel
supremely happy in his embraces and kisses, it is alto-
gether likely that she will be able to enter with him
into the complete realization of the marital experience,
making it a high point of love for both. For the husband the art of sexual love-making is to find the times
when both can enter with splendid abandon into a
passionate expression of their unity and also to discover ways of restraining his impatience until his wife
is ready to experience with him a joyful mutuality of
union.

When the desire of the wife has been aroused she will experience a feeling of keenest delight in her husband and will be ready for complete intercourse. He may effect an entrance with gentleness, then after allowing enough time, a few minutes perhaps, for the organs to become adjusted to each other, he may begin movement slowly so as to avoid premature climax, which a young husband is likely to experience through nervousness.

Rhythm has a part to play in sexual union. The husband almost instinctively finds himself moving and the wife may learn to respond in somewhat the same way. With variation in closeness and contact, and in vigor or activity, perhaps with vigorous thrusting on the husband's part, the two will gradually experience an increasing sense of oneness, of well-being and of pleasure in each other.

They should learn to develop this experience at somewhat the same rate until both can reach a climax of mutual pleasure and release of sex tension in a shared orgasm. This brings a flowing forth of the seminal discharge from the husband which has a soothing influence. In orgasm the wife experiences a series of quick breaths and muscular movements of an involuntary character marking a climax of pleasure, followed by a sense of peace, of well-being, and of joy in union.

This moment in the love of the husband and wife is a most appropriate one for some word of devotion, mutual joy and appreciation. Moreover when this point has been reached the two may still remain together for a little time of gradually lessened lovemaking during which there will be a gradual decline in sex feeling. This period will provide a pleasant aftermath.

Usually the two do nothing to renew sexual passion but rather let it decline gently. Presently they will want to go to sleep, perhaps in each other's arms. Some women, however, experience one or more preliminary orgasms leading up to the final consummation of their sexual self-fulfillment.

In both sexes nature has provided a general pattern of success in marital union and a variety of possible variants of the pattern, and it is highly desirable for both to secure complete expression of sex as provided for in the nervous and glandular system. Chronic sexual dissatisfaction causes a strain on the wife's nerves. It is noteworthy that sexual health and nervous poise are related to each other.

The sex part of life interacts with every other part, being affected by health conditions, by the degree of freshness or fatigue of the individual, by harmony in personal relationships in general, by mental poise and calm, and by the question whether the physical experience is something which is sought merely for itself or whether it is a true expression of love, a culmination of an attitude of mutual self-giving which permeates all the experiences of life.

The first principle is mutuality, that is, to have the sexual expression of married love sought when it can be enjoyed by both. To each it should be a joy generously to meet the sexual needs of the other and this art can be learned more perfectly as time goes on. A good sexual relationship is a part of the pride and joy of a good marriage. It will be found that a finer and more complete experience results from moderation and from great consideration for each other. If the husband and wife seem to differ greatly in their sex needs, they will do well to learn patience. Usually a bride and groom can readily learn to solve their problem and to meet each other's needs. A union in which the husband and wife give themselves wholeheartedly to each other is not only precious to them in the early part of marriage but is likely to remain as a blessing through all their years.

How often complete sexual expression should be added to the every-day endearments is a matter for sensible people to decide in accordance with their own experience. Individuals and couples vary. In Terman's report* already referred to, the great majority of younger couples came within a range from three to twelve times per month, with a few below three and a few above twelve. Frequency declines somewhat with age.

The groom should realize that in the early enthusiasm of marriage it is possible to establish a habit of having union more frequently than would be desirable as a permanent thing. In some cases a wife may

* *Op. cit.*, p. 270.

desire union more frequently than her husband can continue to be organically ready for it.

Sometimes the sexual needs of the wife will seem greater and sometimes those of the husband. The problem for the pair will be to understand each other well enough so that all occasions of such fellowship shall be mutually desired and accompanied by a keen sense of joy in each other.

Many women have a peak of sensitivity just before or just after menstruation, or both before and after. There are some who believe that a more satisfactory marital experience is found by those who unite as they may wish at this time but maintain abstinence at other times. Intercourse just before the middle point between two periods is most likely to result in conception, whereas in the week before the period conception is least likely.

At the beginning of marriage, or if the wife's health is not robust, or during pregnancy it might be better for her to be uppermost or alongside her husband rather than in the usual position on her back. Coitus during pregnancy is often desired. It is necessary, however, that the husband be gentle, avoid undue pressure and stop one to three months before labor is due. He should not impose more weight upon the wife than is pleasing to her.

The couple should experiment freely and use positions best suited to them, approaching this subject without fear or embarrassment. They are made for each other, and will find happiness in giving themselves fully to each other.

In addition to considerations of position and pleasing contacts the married lovers may well give attention to the general aesthetic surroundings, that their high experience of love may be given a pleasing setting, neither in darkness nor in glaring illumination. Having a light, of course, is optional. Above all other things is the need of an atmosphere of mutual appreciation, of love and of peace.

OVERCOMING DIFFICULTIES IN
SEXUAL ADJUSTMENT

Selfishness. Most new couples have at least some difficulty in learning to live unselfishly in the intimacy of marriage. Selfishness impairs all relationships in home life, including the sexual. The unselfish husband thinks of this form of intimacy in its effects upon his wife as much as for his own sake, while the selfish man uses sex as a mere personal gratification, and may only aggravate his mate. He stimulates her sex passion but leaves it unsatisfied, giving her a sense of being abused and exploited rather than loved and treasured. So also the wife may on occasion fail to have sufficient consideration for her mate. Both must learn to love unselfishly or they will never find the fulfillment of love's promise.

An extreme instance of the use of sex in a self-centred way is masturbation. The person who has become addicted to this immature practice and carries it into marriage may be defrauding the mate and making the normal relationship difficult. On the other hand, no one need fear that masturbation in early life may have ruined his chances for an entirely satisfactory adjustment in marriage, or that damage to physical or mental health may have resulted.

Faults of Sexual Approach. By wrong approach the husband may fail to make the marital relationship a means of charming and delighting his wife, but rather may repel her. With a demanding rather than a love-making attitude he neglects to arouse his wife's sexual emotions. From ignorance he passes through a sequence of haste, and clumsiness, causing pain and possible aversion. This can be remedied by attention to his wife's needs and the ways of satisfying them which we have discussed.*

Lack of Control. Another type of difficulty is experienced in a temporary inadequacy of the husband due to nervous fear that he may fail in the new adjustment. He may experience a quick ejaculation of the seminal fluid, after which he may be unable to bring his wife to her orgasm. Since the wife's emotional tide naturally rises more slowly, it is only by learning to delay his orgasm that the husband will be able fully to satisfy her. To learn this may take time, but if he will think of his love rather than his fears, and in the course of experience will seek to discover

---

* In case a fuller discussion is desired, see the list of books at the end of this chapter.

the positions and movements which bring his wife to her culmination while enabling him to delay his own, he will find it possible to lengthen the time of intercourse to their mutual benefit.

The husband will find it desirable to make the entrance gently, to allow a little time for the vagina to adjust itself to his entrance, and to remain quiet for a brief time whenever his own climax approaches before the wife is ready for hers. As the wife develops her true sexual personality, which was dormant in her girlhood, she will be able to have her orgasm more quickly. In the course of a few weeks or months the two who started out requiring dissimilar periods of time will probably find that the wife's culmination can be brought about more quickly, and that of the husband can be delayed. Wives are not necessarily slower than their husbands if the right forms of tactile stimulation are found.

When there is difficulty the two may need to give themselves with greater joy and self-forgetfulness to preliminary love play and mutual petting. On the other hand such difficulty may indicate that they need to devote more attention to the creating of harmony in the other relationships of the home.

The husband should try to have the wife's orgasm beginning before he allows his own to take place. While this may seem impossible to some in their early experience, it can be achieved in time by most. In some cases the husband may continue gentle motion after his orgasm and so bring the wife to hers. He should guard against giving her the feeling that he has left her too soon. If after some months of marriage success seems not to have come, it will be time not to be discouraged but to seek advice, from books or a counselor.

Impotence. Seeming impotence is usually due to nervousness, fear, a wrong emotional attitude, or a wrong program of living. A young bridegroom who was working long hours, feared he was becoming impotent because he was frequently unable to carry intercourse through to mutual consummation. It was pointed out to him that as he was using so much energy in his work and was living a sedentary life, it was unreasonable to suppose that he ought to undertake intercourse as frequently as he had been led to believe. Relief of his worry along with a more sensible program of living brought improvement.

The impotence that some young men fear is usually imaginary. If a man forgets his anxiety and lives an active and wholesome life the need for worry will usually vanish. If not it will be almost certainly curable through the help of a skilled physician. Paradoxically, use of alcohol first accentuates passion and in the end decreases sexual potency. A wife complained that when her husband was under the influence of alcohol he always wanted intercourse but was never able to carry it out.

Frigidity. Usually a woman should experience orgasm at least in a fair proportion of occasions of intercourse. There are some women, however, who are satisfied by well developed responses short of climax.

Women who are constitutionally frigid are few, perhaps one in a hundred, but those who are frigid because of fear, worry or an unhappy attitude toward marital union, are many. Therefore, it is necessary to recognize that there are cases in which the sex life is inadequate because of factors which can be improved. If the sexual experience is unsatisfactory, let the wife reflect that this may be a result of mental bias, and subject to correction. If she were hopelessly frigid she probably would not have loved ardently.

Marion Hilliard, M.D., said that fatigue is the most serious of things that "detract from the happy bedroom." * Physical sex response takes some exuberance, which the over-tired woman or the woman who takes little care of her health may not possess. Fulness and vigor of life are worth cultivating and preserving for many reasons, and for few, if any, more important than that they help the wife and mother to be her best in family life. However, it should be assumed that if sickness should come to either mate the other will show all possible consideration, finding other ways of expressing love and tenderness toward the one who is ill.

Some women experience strong and frequently recurring sex desire† and yet fail of sexual fulfillment

* *Reader's Digest,* April, 1960, p. 69, "Too Tired to Love."
† Cf. *A Research in Marriage,* by G. V. Hamilton. Albert and Charles Boni, New York, p. 543. *Sex Factors in the Life of 2200 Women,* by Katherine Bement Davis, Harper & Brothers, New York.

with their husbands. Such a wife should not necessarily assume that the husband is at fault, though she may need more caressing of the clitoris.

As to mental attitude, though it is difficult by an act of will to change our deep-seated emotional reactions, progress can be made in this also when it is undertaken with patience and understanding. The attitude of love should rule so that fear may be overcome, because love casts out fear.

When Adjustment Is Difficult. In such cases a careful study of their problems, perhaps with the aid of a skilled counselor, would be desirable for both. Dr. Kegel of the University of Southern California Medical School found that a more adequate development of the muscle which supports the organs of the pelvis helps many women to a more complete sexual fulfillment. Exercise to develop this muscle can be carried on by the woman herself. As this muscle controls the flow of urine, a woman by repeatedly stopping the flow and releasing it again will be strengthening this muscle. At the Institute of Family Relations of Los Angeles it was found in a series of one thousand sexually unsatisfied women that sixty-five per cent of them gained relief through the strengthening of this muscle.* Good muscles may be more valuable than many people realize.

In the rare cases in which a fully satisfactory ad-

* See Ronald M. Deutsch, *Reader's Digest.* Oct. 1968, pp. 114–18.

justment is impossible a wise couple will appreciate what their marriage has and work their way forward from that into a more satisfying unity, rather than to feel frustrated because of what they lack. Although they fail of ideal physical adjustment they may find a total sharing of life that is a great joy to them through devotion to their children and such common interests as the home, work, hobbies, friends, social activities, congenial intellectual pursuits, or devotion to art or to religion. The thing for them to do is to cultivate success in other areas rather than to worry when perfect sexual adjustment is lacking.*

The finest and most complete union in a family is the real purpose and aim of marriage. This can be achieved by some to whom perfect sexual union is denied. It is, after all, the entire nature, rather than just the physical nature, that is to be expressed in marriage. While all forms of fulfillment are to be desired, a rich fulfillment on the personality level is the greatest and most enduring reward of a fine marriage. Research studies have shown that personality factors are more important for success in marriage than physical factors. Marriages which do not stop short of the highest goals of understanding, appreciation and comradeship are the ones that hold up best.

* Hamilton, "A Research in Marriage," found some couples reporting that their marriages were successful though complete sexual fulfilment was lacking. Terman, "Psychological Factors in Marital Happiness," found some such cases ranking high in their happiness.

CONTINUANCE OF HARMONIOUS ADJUSTMENT

Successful marital union is not likely to become perfect all at once, but when the marriage is rightly conducted the blending of physical and spiritual elements is such that mutual respect and attraction increase and the two feel inexpressibly dear to each other. Such couples will have no use for divorce courts because to them marriage will be a development rather than a disillusionment, and its preciousness will grow throughout life.

SOME BOOKS THAT HELP IN THE PERSONAL
ADJUSTMENTS OF MARRIAGE

The Intimate Marriage, by HOWARD J. CLINEBELL and CHARLOTTE H. CLINEBELL. Harper and Row.

The Key to Feminine Response in Marriage, by RONALD M. DEUTSCH. Random House.

Sex Fulfilment in Marriage, by ERNEST R. and GLADYS H. GROVES. Emerson Books.

Sex Without Fear, by SAMUEL A. LEWIN and JOHN GILMORE. Lear.

Whom God Hath Joined, by DAVID MACE. Westminster Press.

Sexual Pleasure in Marriage, by JEROME and JULIA RAINER. Julian Messner, Inc.

Understanding Each Other, by PAUL TOURNIER. John Knox Press.

Chapter V

MEETING DIFFICULTIES CONSTRUCTIVELY

EVERY FAMILY HAS difficulties to meet and no two couples are just alike in their problems or in their adjustments. Some have their greatest difficulties in one realm and some in another. Certain families have a fine degree of adjustment in every aspect of life, while others at times become maladjusted at almost every point. Many have periods of harmony interspersed with experiences of discord. When issues arise it is of great value if members can learn to meet them constructively, letting their love inspire them to work through each difficulty to a better understanding.

Every test which we meet successfully makes us better prepared to meet the next one. The difference between marriages which make a fine success and those which fall short is not that the latter have problems while the former have none, but that the marriages which succeed splendidly are those in which the members approach each question with patience and with loyal determination to find the answer. In such a spirit many difficult problems can be solved or outgrown.

The family which fails to gain happiness in marriage is often one which allows little grievances to accumulate until the skies of love are overcast, and fear, doubt and antagonism creep in.

The person who is learning to see life as a married person, rather than as an individualist, will ask: "How can this particular situation be used for the good of our home?" In single life a person can be "I-minded" and get away with it, although not well, but a married person must become "we-minded." Each must feel that the other is on his side and not against him. This is the situation in true marriage. Many of the troubles of family life are caused by using the single person's approach in the married person's situation.

DISAGREEMENTS

Differences in a family are differences within a unity. The united mind of the two is wiser than the mind of either individual. Each can learn from the other, and when disagreements occur both should work back from the particular difference to the essential harmony which unites. A marriage is not like a debating society, in which the aim is to win against the other side, but a team in which the two need to learn how best to pull together.

Characters do not change magically at the marriage altar, and any two people who establish a home together take into it some roots of disagreement. When such disagreements arise they should not be taken too seriously, nor should the one resent the fact that the other has a different point of view. Differences may become stepping stones to finer adjustments or they may be turned into occasions of petty quarreling. In the latter case the two exhaust themselves pulling against each other. Don't keep your mate on the defensive or rub sore spots.

The strength of marriage is in harmony. Determination to carry one's point or to "see who is boss," is a form of pride and selfishness. But as the love of dominating others is a weakness quite common to human nature the married person must guard against it. A person with an extreme love of argument must keep this under control, unless both can take pleasure in debate and come out happier. A great danger is for a partner who loves arguments to keep them going with a mate who dislikes them. However unreasonable the mate's position may seem he cannot change his point of view on command. To carry on a one-sided argument tenaciously is a form of nagging, a thing which nobody likes. When conflict comes each should be big enough to think somewhat like this: "Although my mate's point of view seems wrong to me, yet his way of thinking must be important to him. We must work out a better understanding."

A quarrel is not usually a case of one fully right and the other all wrong, but both seeing a question somewhat out of perspective because they are excited. By letting the matter rest a little each should presently get more insight into the merits of the position of the other, and a little less cocksureness about his own position.

When an argument arises if both will take the position of objective observers, asking what is happening and why, the situation will sometimes look ridiculous and both can laugh together. At other times the issue will be a real one but better met by further study of the question than by the clash of antagonism.

Disagreements are a part of the common experience of humanity, married or single. Many of them arise because people misunderstand one another, because they take some word or act in a way that was never intended, or because they are over sensitive. Most clashes are preventable, especially in marriage. It has been said that nine-tenths of human misery is mere nonsense.* Equally it should be realized that most of the things that cause difficulty in the home are trivial in comparison with the great things on which the husband and wife agree, so each should be, within reason, a rooter for the other.

The late Dr. Ernest R. Groves, who helped many thousands of families to a finer success, advised the young wife to try to work out of every spat into a fuller appreciation of her husband's needs, to learn to look for his reasons and to make herself big enough to understand and tolerate them. Then, of course he gave similar advice to young men.

* The Happy Family, by Dr. John Levy and Dr. Ruth Munroe, Knopf, New York.

Permanent differences in temperament and outlook may be accepted in the realization that there are deeper joys and harmonies which more than compensate. Couples should look upon their differences as part of the exquisitely delicate adjustment that human personality requires. Among the finest marriages are some in which really difficult adjustments are made for the sake of a higher unity.

EMOTIONAL UPSETS

People who learn not to give way to emotional tantrums are more successful in marriage. Angry behavior, which is considered crude in any social group, is even more out of place for those who love. The realization of this will prevent much misery on both sides. Tennyson in his poem "The First Quarrel" shows in a startling way how anger may distort the mind with a hard and dangerous bitterness.

Often people act on impulses of which they are not fully aware, their emotions disturbed by unrecognized causes. Because we are experiencing some inner tension we take it out on someone else, and the marriage partner is likely to be the one. If we suffer from loneliness, jealousy, lack of self-confidence or frustration, the inner condition puts into our words and acts a tension that may be quite out of accord with the real love which we have in our hearts.

Moreover, we may flare up over some little thing, mainly because it sets off some old habit of irritation. In childhood, perhaps, we were compelled by some person whom we did not like to wear rubbers at play; then on a damp morning wife lovingly insists that we wear them to the office. Before we know it the old habit of irritation has flared up and wife is hurt by the way we answer. It is absurd, of course, for us to act that way but such unconscious influences are often at the roots of our behavior.

Other unrecognized sources of emotional flare-ups are in the unpleasant experiences that people have out in the world. Without being aware of it, they sometimes carry the emotional results into their home life. A woman has had an unpleasant experience in a store, or a man has gone through a difficult half-hour with the boss. There was indignation but it could not be expressed at the time. Such a person is ready to become annoyed over some trifle in the home. Sometimes, before we know it, we fly off the handle.

Some families have difficulties because it is hard for them to adjust to the real world of practical married love. When their love was in a dream world they did not give thought to the fact that marriage would have such unpleasant things as bills to pay or leaky water pipes or a TV set out of order. It all seems so different from their romantic dreams, and one may unconsciously take out his resentment on the other.

Married people should realize that most of the flare-ups of the home are not really serious. We should be mature enough to use them constructively as an opportunity for growth or, better still, we should be thoughtful enough to prevent them, as far as possible. Bitter things said may be hard to live down. In such a case silence is golden.

The husband and wife should realize in advance that if they find themselves occasionally at odds it will not mean that they are unsuited to each other but rather that they need to learn some new lesson in cooperation. Sometimes, like mountain climbers, they will be safer because they are tied together. Scaling the heights with greatest care, they will be rewarded by a happy feeling of accomplishment and a new vision.

People who want to do everything to build up their marriage and nothing to endanger it will cultivate every habit and custom which adds pleasure and so helps to keep a stream of satisfactory happenings flowing through the daily life.

WHAT ABOUT INCOMPATIBILITY?

Faults of adjustment should not be a cause of fear, yet "incompatibility" is a scare that frightens people. It sounds rather hopeless. Often it is really no more than a way of saying that the persons involved are selfish and unwilling to make concessions. Sometimes it means that they are too ignorant to carry out their physical mating with a reasonable degree of harmony

Few are the pairs who cannot achieve harmony, both sexual and mental, if they are willing to give themselves fully and unselfishly to each other.

There is a growing understanding that incompatibility is not so much a necessary clash between two natures as it is a result of wrong training or a condition that people bring upon themselves, while compatibility is a happy state that married people gain by whole-hearted and intelligent effort. It may be aided by good training and fortunate choice but it is not merely an accident. Seeming incompatibility can be corrected in many cases by studying how to lessen misunderstandings and annoyances, and how to grow in patience and mutual self-giving.

If people begin to rub each other the wrong way a change of subject and of interest will often help, or perhaps a change of scene. Even those who love may see each other too much and others too little. Seeing other friends and places helps to restore perspective so that the molehills that looked like mountains are cut down to size, and the two can be all the happier because they see things in their true proportions again.

WHAT IS SUCCESSFUL MARRIAGE?

When married lovers return from the honeymoon they take up together the task of making a home. Now, although they are not less lovers than before, their love must be seasoned with more of the practical, and each must learn to think of the daily duties as a part of their expression of regard for each other.

The romantic wife may wish the honeymoon could have continued, and may be tempted to resent the requirements of her husband's calling which inevitably make heavy demands upon his time. She must realize, however, that a new phase of being lovers is their being homemakers together. They must cultivate the art of being lovers and homemakers as they have previously found the thrills of being dates, sweethearts, and honeymooners.

The two should now study to create a mutually satisfying program of living. Their marriage can be really successful in the highest sense only if it is thoroughly satisfactory to both. One of the wife's main duties is to help her husband achieve a successful career as a man and a husband, and equally the husband has a responsibility for helping the wife achieve a satisfying career as a woman and a wife. In this way their development in personality will be on a high level and their marriage will have a built-in security.

A successful marriage is not merely one which holds together and keeps away from the divorce court, but one whose members find zest in living and have not only respect but enthusiasm for each other. Happiness is a matter of knowing where to place the emphasis, distinguishing between the major and minor goals and between the minor and major domestic virtues. It is a matter of confidence, of being clean, wholesome, attractive and interesting and of giving love without measure.

Married love is related to courtship as a larger tree is related to the smaller one that it once was. As time goes on the tree puts on new rings of growth, sends its roots deeper into the soil and bears flowers and fruit which it could not bear before. The transition from romantic love to married love does not take place so automatically but under the warm sun of mutual love and effort, it, too, may grow sturdier from year to year.

Every marriage should have three kinds of love: 1) romantic, keeping alive something of the zest and sparkle and "special-ness" of courtship days, 2) domestic, weaving the mutual concern and passionate kindness of the two into a pattern of living, and 3) a love like the love of God which holds steady even when people are at their worst, and is always ready to forgive. We marry "for better or for worse" and if the worse comes we must sometimes take it with patience and kindness. Love is by nature a courageous and hopeful thing. It defies definition yet makes life more meaningful, creates a spring of happiness within us, and enables marriage to triumph over many obstacles, even the bitter obstacle of harsh circumstances that separate the two for a time, because it still has its strong inner ties which bind the two together, and

their love is a part of their very being; while they live
for the time when they can be together again.

We do not think of marriage as a series of question marks representing this and that adjustment, but
as a series of plus signs which increase the joys of life
and lessen its sorrows. The partner is to be thought
of not merely as a person to whom we must adjust,
but much more as one who enters with us into the
fuller joys of living. Marriage out of adjustment is
agony, but kept in good repair it is a perennial joy.
Where there are differences a 50-50 principle will
usually bridge them, but a 60-60 attitude is even
better. Adjustments will be made and each will feel
married to a very reasonable and considerate person.

Chapter VI

PARENTHOOD

THE JOYS AND responsibilities of parenthood enrich family experience and bring the particular couple into the endless process of renewing the life of the human race. The world is constantly being fashioned and re-fashioned in its homes. To say that the social virtues of tenderness, responsibility, sympathy and devotion have their roots in parental experience is true and important, but pale compared with the radiant joy that parents have in the renewal of themselves and their love in their children. In the family plan therefore children should have a central place. It brings greater joy to spend money for children than for an expensive manner of living. A part of growth in marriage is growth into parenthood.

PREGNANCY

A mother of a fine family says, "While there are old wives and some young ones who shake their heads and sympathize with the pregnant young woman, there are others who have passed through the experience with a sense of high adventure and achievement. When we tell her that she is entering a creative, vivid adventure, where in spite of physical ills she can walk on air for pure joy, we tell her the truth if she will but turn her face that way. Let her experience the joy of passing on through her body a torch of life that comes from endless ages and will go on infinitely. That is rising to the heights of life on the dramatic level."

The experiences of parenthood tend to keep parents young and vital. To be a mother of a suitable number of children is good for the physical and emotional health of a wife: women who have none are more likely to suffer from nervous ills.

BIRTH REGULATION AND BIRTH RELEASE

As parenthood is too sacred to be undertaken irresponsibly. the problem for the married pair is the spacing of pregnancy, not its undue avoidance. All couples will desire to select the best time to start each of the pregnancies with due regard to the health of the mother and children, and the welfare of the whole family.

Starting a family before the home is settled is usually unwise. If time is allowed for the husband and wife to work out the details of daily living, their future happiness is more likely to be based on clear and considerate understanding than if from the beginning the care required for the pregnant wife has to affect all their actions. Except when the wife is well past thirty or the couple is wealthy, postponement of pregnancy for six months or a year usually works out best. Then for the well-being of children an adequate spacing perhaps eighteen to thirty months apart is usually better. When there are as many children as wisdom dictates, again protection against unwise pregnancy may be needed.

Protection—that is, contraception—should be undertaken, not on the basis of what some friend has found successful, or of some advertisement, but by advice of a physician who has the necessary special knowledge, or of a birth control clinic or maternal health agency. The accredited methods of adequately trained doctors and clinics are harmless, and do not produce unfavorable after-effects, as results in many thousands of cases have proven. They remove that sense of apprehension which mars the peace of marital union for many couples.

Those who have been taught that no method but the observance of the "safe period" is right may make a study for several months with a calendar on which the date of each period is marked, or the wife may record her temperature on arising each day for several months, as body temperature rises slightly at ovulation. Then she may get medical advice as to whether she can depend on her regularity. One difficulty is that many women do not produce the egg always on the usual calendar date, so it is possible that ovulation and conception may take place at an unexpected time.

Although refraining from intercourse is sometimes

suggested when the two are not ready for a child, this may put an unnecessary strain on both, and may have undesired side effects on the unity and emotional health of both. Hence birth control by sound methods under good medical guidance is preferable in most families.

If there is an unforeseen pregnancy it should not be treated as a misfortune, for the coming of the child may result in unforeseen happiness for the family. It is especially necessary for the sake of the child's emotional health, that he should have the sense of being wanted and treasured by his parents. If they regard him as an unwelcomed burden, it destroys his emotional security and puts a weight upon his mind which is likely to bear him down. Every child has the right to be wanted. At the opposite extreme are those tragic cases in which people resort to abortion, without adequate ethical guidance or skilled medical care, when conception has taken place and there is unwillingness to have the child.

ANTICIPATION OF PARENTHOOD

The expectant mother should be under the guidance of a good physician from the time pregnancy is discovered. Care should be taken to practice moderation in the sex relationship and to avoid it entirely at the period when menstruation would normally have taken place, because of the greater liability of the wife to miscarriage at such times.

The husband is to realize that his wife is under nervous and emotional tensions which call for patience and sympathy on his part. If at this time a wife should feel a sudden and unexplained aversion to her mate, both of them should know that it is a result of her condition rather than a real change in her attitude. Failing to realize this some young people have drifted into unpleasant and bitter experiences of misunderstanding entirely out of harmony with their love for each other. Sometimes this happens partly because the nature of the wife calls out all the more at this time, in a way which she may not fully understand, for the full sympathy and support of her husband. If he will help her through the early part of this period by unusual considerateness he will be likely to find that health and happiness are improved, as her whole being meets the call of motherhood.

Anticipation and realization of fatherhood and motherhood deepen love and add to happiness. The parents have united physically to give life to the child. Now they must unite all that is in them to give the best nurture and guidance. They give the gift of themselves to their children, sharing the treasures of love with new lives, and broadening and deepening the range of experience together.

Through parenthood they achieve more complete expression of the full sex nature of each. This, in the man, leads him to wish to make a home for the loved mate, and to unite with her in building a good family. It shows itself also in the tender solicitude of the father toward the little child, and the desire to shape the environment in such a way that his home and family may be secure and happy. Similarly on the part of the woman, her complete sexual personality leads her to desire to be an ideal wife, and gives her the inexpressible tenderness and strength of motherhood. There is no finer achievement in which a man and woman can share than the creation of a good family. Mother love is a foundation for a child's emotional security, while father love is needed as a strong support and background. Such love reaches out toward other families also, with a desire that the world may be a suitable place for the homes of all people.

CREATING A FAVORABLE ATMOSPHERE FOR CHILDREN

The family at its best is a training school of personality, with joy in work and play, unity in aims and ideals, self-confidence, and deep gratifications of each member in being able to give joy to the ones most dear. Such a home creates an atmosphere favorable to the happy development of children.

Young couples do better not to wait too long before having children, lest there should be too great a distance between the generations.

It is a benefit to the child to have brothers and sisters near his own age because they become playmates, share experiences and help one another in personality development. An only child is likely to have too much parental emotion centered upon him, whether of pleasure or dissatisfaction. As a result, he may not adjust himself happily in the world of his equals where he must make his place. He must not be given the feeling that the world revolves around him, but must learn to be a person among persons in the give and take of life.

For the problems of pregnancy and parenthood it is well to take advantage of helpful books which are available in all good libraries, and to possess the most helpful ones if possible. Some excellent free pamphlets on child training can be secured from the Children's Bureau in Washington. It is well for people to anticipate parenthood, to draw in advance upon the best wisdom available and to plan for children not only in terms of health and support, but also of family happiness and the sharing of love.

Giving the child a good start physically becomes easier if he is nursed by his mother. This should be considered by all mothers because they want of course to do everything possible for their children.

A certain proportion of married folk find that they do not have as many children as they want. Such people ought not to give up hope, however, for a considerable number, who would otherwise be childless, can have their hope for children fulfilled through modern medical help. Physicians and planned parenthood leagues offer fertility services as well as help in the spacing of pregnancies.

For married couples to have an average of three children will maintain the population at its present level, and most people want children for the completion of their family life, and at the same time they want to make a good contribution to the next generation of the world.

The joys of parenthood are enhanced by the thought of building a better future for children and through them. To rear a new generation with the highest ideals, and in accordance with the best procedures in child training, gives to the homemaking task the dignity of an art and a noble profession.

The human race has gone far toward conquering the forces of earth, sea and air, but the advances of the past and present can be crowned with most complete fulfillment only by rising to a level of human living to match, and make best use of, our material achievements. When we consider the way in which the spirit of man presses forward to reach new heights, we would be faint-hearted if we did not dare to dream of a nobler future for our children, and, in spite of all discouragements, to work with them for a happy and peaceful world.

This better future, however, can not be built without secure foundations in home life. As we think of the millions of homes in all parts of the country, on busy city streets, in pleasant suburbs, by lake or stream, or on sun-streaked hillsides, do we not see in these more than anywhere else, the very heart of our nation's life? If we picture fathers returning home with gladness, met by smiling eyes of women, gathering in home circles amid the romping of children, and if we contemplate all the joy and good will that are constantly being generated in family life, do we not see in and through the home a possibility of building a world on sounder, saner principles, and of creating a type of human life nearer to the heart's desire? Even the peace of the community, the nation, and the world can be advanced by the attitudes developed in our families. People who live in harmony at home add to the peace of the world, and children brought up in such homes can be so conditioned and trained that they will go out into the world blessed with the attitudes of peacemakers, and with skill in promoting harmonious relations. For the kind of life and the kind of world we want we must make it possible for families everywhere to create good homes, and must eliminate the root causes of bitterness, so that families may live in peace and the human race, living in an unpolluted environment with good will one to another, may be the true family of God.

Chapter VII

THE DEEPER MEANING
OF MARRIAGE

LIFE AT ITS best is a spiritual venture having a supreme goal and purpose. Our fellowship with one another is most complete when together we realize that the foundations of our marriage, as of our being, are in God, who is the greater Love beyond, beneath and within our human love.

THE HIGHER NEEDS

Persons become unhappy when they fail to meet the needs of the higher side of their nature. Man cannot live by bread alone, and a family cannot live in material things alone. Deep in the heart are spiritual needs which are like hunger and thirst, the repression of which throws life out of balance and robs it of its richest meaning.

We need to be adjusted not only to one another but to life and to God. Every family needs a dynamic of conviction and an ultimate goal for its striving. Religion focuses these values and represents the spirit of love in its highest and most practical sense.

If we give careful thought to the foundations, our homes will be more secure. There will also be the satisfaction of feeling that our home is a part of

God's kingdom on earth. It adds immensely to the joy of homemaking to realize that when we build with God His laws help us in preserving and increasing the happiness of the home.

There is something about living with God, who is love, which gives a fuller splendor to our family relationships. When parenthood comes the parents stand in the place of God to the little child. In order to be prepared for such a responsibility they need, of course, to have God in the home before the children arrive.

Religion is a means of laying hold upon a wisdom greater than our own as we look to the objectives of the voyage which we are taking. It does not mean forgetting daily concerns in order to concentrate upon God, but finding God, like light and power in the midst of all our relationships. "A flash of gorgeous knowledge of the presence and beauty of God may come through some earthly love, that life-giving emotion which makes us part of the Creator and bestows a cosmic consciousness that links us with all creation." * Something of this consciousness was expressed in the words of a husband who said to his wife, "In your eyes, my darling, I have seen the Infinite."

COMPLETE LOVE

The great principles of religion are aids to family

* Frank D. Getty, in I. H. Smith, *Are You Ready for Marriage?* Liveright, New York, p. 197.

happiness. The first and greatest of the commandments is: "Thou shalt love the Lord thy God with
all thy heart, and with all thy soul, and with all thy
mind, and with all thy strength," and the second is,
"Thou shalt love thy neighbor as thyself." * If we
catch the spirit of these words we may apply the
same thought to the relationships of husbands and
wives: thou shalt love thy mate as thyself, and more
than thyself—love with all the heart, the emotional
nature; all the mind, the intellectual nature; all the
soul, the æsthetic and religious nature; and all the
strength, combining physical, emotional, intellectual
and spiritual qualities in a whole-hearted devotion.

The words of Jesus, "A new commandment I
give to you, that you love one another; even as I have
loved you," † are as helpful as if they had been uttered
for husbands and wives.

What does it mean to love as Christ loved? It
means that our love is to develop the qualities that
his love showed—understanding, seeing into the
heart; appreciation, seeing the best in people; unsel-
fishness, a concern for the happiness of the other,
a forgiving spirit in which he gave an example that
the world can never forget, and finding God close
to us in our love for one another.

Love within the home prepares us better to love

* Mark 12:30–31.
† John 13:34. Revised Standard Version. Used by permission
of the National Council of Churches.

our neighbors. The attitude of loving one's neighbor as oneself creates a kindlier atmosphere, brings one into a larger circle of good will, and develops character in such a way that the home is benefited. It means growth in kindness, fairness, and ability to help others to be their best. It means spreading the influences of fellowship and good will all about us, and unloading any grudges and bitternesses that we may have. These bring a sad harvest, but "The harvest of the Spirit is love, joy, peace, good temper, kindliness, generosity, fidelity, gentleness, self-control." * Every one of these qualities will develop in a home that gives due place to the spiritual life.

A SACRED UNDERTAKING

High hopes of excellence in their life together are normal to young people in love. As husband and wife they need faith in God, and in the sacredness of their undertaking. In a world where there are many lives that simply drift, they should have a purpose. The person who starts with a conviction that the task of building a home is worthy of high devotion is likely to be an individual worth living with, while the cynical mind that does not believe supremely in anything is a handicap in marriage.

People starting out on the journey together most naturally turn to God in prayer for the success of their

* Galatians 5:22–23, Moffatt's Translation. Used by permission of Harper and Brothers, N. Y.

venture. When they become parents they can hardly think without awe and tenderness of the life which they have brought into the world. And when it comes to the early training of children, what is more desirable than to create a family atmosphere charged with faith and love? Family members living without thought of spiritual things are like dwellers in a valley who never lift up their eyes to the mountain tops.

RELIGION AND PERSONAL CHARACTER

Religion at its best brings out in people those attitudes which make family life worthy and inspiring. In helping people to be upright, loyal, unselfish, patient, courageous, and also easier to live with, true religion aids in the development of the finest home-making qualities.

These qualities are favorable to the continuance of mutual respect and admiration. At the time of marriage each has, of course, the full respect of the other and it is one of the most precious assets. If at any time mutual respect is damaged in any degree it must be re-established as quickly and as fully as possible, because respect is a necessary ingredient of love.

William Lyon Phelps, a great teacher and a keen observer of family life, said: "Since the greatest of all arts is the art of living together, and since the highest and most permanent happiness depends on it, and since the way to practice this art successfully lies through character, the all important question is how to obtain character. The surest way is through religion in the home." * This is a most reasonable statement because religion which is the experience of the love of God in the home is a corrective for our faults and a means of strengthening our good points. The New Testament says: "Whatever is true, whatever is honorable, whatever is just, whatever is pure, whatever is lovely, whatever is gracious; if there is any excellence, if there is anything worthy of praise, think about these things." † Here also we find great wisdom for family experience. It means that as we live together we cultivate the attitude of appreciation rather than criticism and learn to find the best in one another.

We know that there is a personal discipline which prepares the way for the highest achievements of the athlete or the musician. There is also a spiritual discipline which aids the highest living in personal and family experience. Commonplace living is easy, but the finest living calls for our very best and nothing less than this is good enough for our homes.

RELIGION SHARED IN THE HOME

The religious life of the home should be higher and deeper than all creeds or ceremonies, as the husband and wife share in their thinking about the truth,

* By permission of Good Housekeeping Magazine.
† Phil. 4:8. Revised Standard Version. Used by permission of the National Council of Churches.

beauty and love that are beyond and within all things, and as they look upon the tragedies of the world. Their religion must not be a formality which they go through, careless-hearted and uninspired, for the real religion of the home is the sum and substance of its highest ideals and of its deepest love.

"Religion at its best burns like an altar fire in the home and God is the unseen guest day and night. Such an experience may seem difficult of realization, and it is, but not so difficult as appears. It requires daily consecration, daily thoughtfulness and daily 'practice of the Presence of God.' . . . Long experience has shown that the home is more stable when the husband and wife keep their ideals by God's strength; when children learn to pray at their mother's knee; when the family go to church together as a family custom and as a conscious participation in community life. The child needs the divinest home earth can offer. He thrives best in settled ways, where life is on a high plane. He lives by love as much as by food and drink." *

What is said here about the child is equally true of grown people. The world is sometimes cold. We need our hearts warmed at home. When life is hard we need a refuge where our strength can be restored. The parent also, or the newly married person, lives by love as much as by food and drink.

* *Christian Marriage,* Commission on Marriage and the Home, Federal Council of Churches, p. 13.

Practical results of religion in family success have been indicated in a striking way in a number of studies that have been made. These have shown that divorce is rare in homes in which the husband and wife take their church duties seriously. Time taken for private and family prayer and for public worship is time spent in building up the spiritual strength of the family. These habits bring the family into an atmosphere in which appreciation, forbearance and mutual devotion are cultivated, and a critical and unforgiving spirit is out of place.

One would say to homemakers: "Never let religion be an occasion for unkindness, intolerance, or prejudice against each other, or against any human soul. Honor all good people, whether of your creed or of some other. So far as you have ability and opportunity, work with all who in any way are striving to advance human good. Your family is part of a world of families. Help lift the general level.

"If creeds and forms presented to you as embodying religion do not satisfy you, look for the truth and beauty that are deeper than all forms. If your church is imperfect try to make it more perfect through your influence in it. Do not throw stones of criticism at those who are trying to make the world better. Help them, and carry on a demonstration of human betterment at home."

The great and wonderful stream of life comes out of the past and flows through us toward future generations. We are heirs of all the ages yet we must take up our inheritance and prepare to pass it on not only unimpaired but built up and revitalized. If in our familes we work together, with devotion to each other, with reverence for the great gift of life, and in harmony with God, we shall not fail to find the highest possible good.

Chapter VIII

PATHWAYS TO HARMONY OF SPIRIT

When a family cares enough about spiritual things to incorporate them in its life the home will gain a sense of high fellowship. A daily recognition of the spiritual is like looking up at the stars. Each family will shape its own program of religious expression, probably with some elements adapted from the childhood homes of the two, and others worked out in their own experience.

A HOME DEDICATION SERVICE

The new custom of dedicating homes places an emphasis on the sacredness of the home and on the distinctness of the new family.

The dedication service offered here can be conducted by homemakers, either by themselves or with any others they may desire to have present. Parts of it may be assigned to the pastor or others. The parts are here divided between the husband and wife.

Musical Prelude. (*Optional*)

Recognition

Husband: "Behold I stand at the door and knock; if any man hear my voice and open the door, I will come in."

Wife: We recognize Christ as the head of this house, its Guest and also its Lord.

A Beatitude for the Family*

Happy is the family that has a true home built by loyal hearts,
For home is not a dwelling but a living fellowship,
In love and understanding.
And happy is the family whose members find a deeper unity
In sharing truth and beauty and devotion to the good.
Their love shall be an altar fire
Burning in the temple of the Highest.

Prayer

O God our Father, and our eternal Friend, we recognize with joy that thou art the Source and Giver of the love that draws us together. We pray that Thou wilt be present in this home, that Thy love may enrich its fellowships, Thy wisdom be its guide, Thy truth its light and Thy peace its benediction, through Jesus Christ our Lord.

* Parts may be assigned and adapted. If the minister is present he may be asked to take certain parts. Music may be woven in or there may be a moment of silence here or there.

House Blessing. (May be repeated in unison, or responsively.)

> "Bless the four corners of this house
> And be the lintel blest,
> And bless the hearth and bless the board,
> And bless each place of rest;
>
> And bless the door that opens wide
> To stranger as to kin
> And bless each crystal window-pane
> That lets the starlight in;
>
> And bless the roof-tree overhead
> And every sturdy wall.
> The peace of man, the peace of God,
> The peace of love o'er all." *

Scripture†

A new commandment I give to you, that you love one another; even as I have loved you, that you also love one another. By this all men will know that you are my disciples, if you have love for one another. (John 13:34, 35.)

Love is patient and kind; love is not jealous or boastful; it is not arrogant or rude. Love does not insist on its own way; it is not irritable or resentful; it does not rejoice at wrong, but rejoices in the right. Love bears all things, believes all things, hopes all things, endures all things. (I CORINTHIANS 13:4–7.)

* Arthur Guiterman, *Death and General Putnam and 101 Other Poems.* E. P. Dutton & Co., Inc., New York, N. Y. Used by permission.
† Revised Standard Version of the Bible. Used by permission of the National Council of Churches

Hymn.* "For the Beauty of the Earth."

For the beauty of the earth,
For the beauty of the skies,
For the love which from our birth
Over and around us lies,
    Lord of All, to Thee we raise
    This our hymn of grateful praise.

For the joy of human love,
Brother, sister, parent, child,
Friends on earth and friends above,
For all gentle thoughts and mild,
    Lord of All, to Thee we raise
    This our hymn of grateful praise.

—CONRAD KOCHER

Declaration

Husband: We who make up this family believe that God
        has brought us together and that He is our Helper.
Wife: We agree to work and pray that our home may
        be a source of strength to its members and a place
        of warmth and fellowship to all who come into it.

Dedication and Candle-Lighting Ceremony
(Parts divided as desired.)

We dedicate our home to love and understanding.
May its joys and sorrows be shared and the individuality
of each member appreciated.

We light a candle to F A M I L Y   L O V E

We dedicate our home to work and leisure. May it

* Other hymns may be chosen as desired.

have gaiety and high fellowship, with kindness in its voices and laughter ringing within its walls.

We light a candle to H A P P I N E S S

We dedicate our home to a friendly life. May its doors open in hospitality and its windows look out with kindness toward other homes.

We light a candle to F R I E N D S H I P

We dedicate our home to cooperation. May its duties be performed in love, its furnishings bear witness that the work of others ministers to our comfort and its table remind us that the work of many people helps supply our needs.

We light a candle to C O O P E R A T I O N

We dedicate our home to the appreciation of all things true and good. May our books bring wisdom, our pictures symbolize things beautiful and our music bring joy and inspiration.

We light a candle to A P P R E C I A T I O N

We dedicate our time and talents to live for one another, to serve our generation and to help build a world in which every family may have a home of comfort and fellowship.

We light a candle to U N S E L F I S H S E R V I C E

We dedicate our home as a unit in the church universal, an instrument of the kingdom of God, a place for worship and Christian training and a threshold to the life eternal.

We light a candle to S P I R I T U A L E N R I C H - M E N T

If there is a fireplace the husband may light a fire and all present throw twigs on it.

Husband: As the flames point upward so our thoughts rise in gratitude to God for this home, and in prayer for His blessing upon it.

Prayer of Dedication. (Followed by the Lord's Prayer, all uniting.)

O God, our Father, we thank Thee for this home, and for those other homes whose good influences remain with us. Help us so to live together here that Thy blessing may rest upon us and Thy joy be in our hearts. As we grow in love and comradeship may our thoughts go out in good will to our neighbors and to all mankind, and more and more may we know Thy love which passes all understanding.

As we dedicate this home we pray that Thou wilt consecrate it by Thine own indwelling, that its light may so shine before men that they shall glorify Thee, through Jesus Christ our Lord who taught us to pray:

Our Father—

Solo or Reading, "Bless This House" by Helen Taylor.*

Bless this house, O Lord we pray,
Make it safe by night and day;
Bless these walls, so firm and stout;
Keeping want and trouble out;
Bless the roof and chimney tall,

* Reprinted by permission of the copyright owners, Boosey and Hawkes, Inc., 30 West 57th Street, New York, N. Y.

Let Thy peace lie over all;
Bless this door that it may prove
Ever open to joy and love.

Bless these windows shining bright,
Letting in God's heavenly light;
Bless the hearth a-blazing there,
With smoke ascending like a prayer;
Bless the folk who dwell within,
Keep them pure and free from sin;
Bless us all that we may be,
Fit O Lord to dwell with Thee.

Benediction

"The Lord bless us and keep us, the Lord make his face to shine upon us and be gracious unto us, the Lord lift up His countenance upon us and give us peace. Amen."

Closing Moment of Silent Prayer.
(Soft music if desired.)

If guests are present the occasion should now lose all formality and everyone should be made to feel very much at home. A song fest of old favorites would be in order, if desired; or one or more solos if persons present are prepared for them. When the two are alone they will express their love to each other with joy and gaiety, for the home is their honeymoon continued.

GRACE AT TABLE

At meals together in the cozy intimacy of the new

home, there is no finer custom than grace at table. It will be most natural for the husband and wife partaking of their daily food at their own table to look to God in gratitude. Then later when children have come into the family a little circle joining hands and bowing around the table will be a pleasing sight.

The following forms of grace are offered by way of suggestion:

We give thanks to Thee, our Father, for this food provided for our returning needs, and for all the hands that have helped to prepare it for our table. Bless them and us, in Jesus' name. Amen.

For what we are about to receive may the Lord make us truly thankful, through Jesus Christ our Lord, Amen.

God bless thy gifts to our use and us in thy service, through Christ our Lord. Amen.

Give us grateful hearts, our Father, for all thy gifts to us, and make us thoughtful of the needs of others. Amen.

PRAYER IN THE HOME

Prayers for the home should enter into its hopes, joys, sorrows, struggles and triumphs. On occasion the members will pray wholeheartedly in connection with some special need. The pair who pray will lay hold on sources of power and of understanding greater than their own, and will gain for their home something of the strength and serenity of God, Himself.

Jesus, giving us a prayer which his followers have used for nearly two thousand years and in all parts of the world, made it a model of trust in God and devotion to his kingdom. The Lord's Prayer is about the most suitable one that could be imagined. It assumes the unity of the group and is concerned with common needs and with our relationships with our fellows; and it fits all these into their place in the program of the eternal kingdom of God. When we use the Lord's Prayer, and we should use it often in the home, let us guard against the carelessness of familiarity and seek to renew in our lives the spirit of Jesus who taught us so to pray.

Other prayers some or all of which might be helpful in any family are given here. Sometimes one of these being used as a start, the family will want to add special petitions of its own. These prayers may be followed by the Lord's Prayer.

Let the words of my mouth and the meditation of my heart, be acceptable in thy sight, O Lord, my strength and my redeemer.*

O God, we have no words sufficient to thank Thee for the great good which comes into our lives: but we pray that we may glorify Thee with cheerful hearts, and by lives which reveal thy goodness to others. Amen.

O God, our Father, make our home a part of thy true kingdom. May thy kindness be in our voices, thy love in our eyes, and thy purposes in our works. And may this

* Ps. 19:14.

day which thou hast given us be a part of our life in Thee. Amen.

O God, our Father, we thank Thee for health of body and of mind, for beautiful things in thy world, and the appeal of things unseen. Help us this day to be in harmony with thy purposes and to be our best for each other and for Thee. Through Christ our Lord. Amen.

Our Lord, who art our strength and whose service is our highest joy; save us from holding too dear the things that pass away, and too cheap the things which are eternal. Enrich us with thy true riches; save us from pride, self-seeking and fear, and give us the spirit of Christ our Lord, whose service is perfect freedom. Amen.

Direct us, O Lord, with thy most gracious favor, and further us with thy continual help, that in all our works, begun, continued and ended in Thee, we may glorify thy holy name, through Jesus Christ our Lord. Amen.*

As we leave our home in thy strength, Our Father, help us wherever we go to carry the spirit of love, and to do to others as we would have them do to us. And so through this day may we serve Thee with true hearts, and live and move and have our being in Thee. Amen.

O God, our Father and our eternal Friend, we thank Thee for our home, a shelter for love and a haven from the turmoil of the world. Within these walls, and even more within our hearts, may we have Thee as our divine Guest, that thy goodness may bless our lives, and thy love cast out every fear, through Christ our Lord, Amen.

Eternal God, light of the minds that know Thee, joy of

* Adapted from the Book of Common Prayer. New York, Oxford U. Press, p. 556.

the hearts that love Thee, and strength of the wills that serve Thee; grant us so to know Thee that we may truly love Thee, so to love that we may fully serve Thee, to the honor and glory of thy holy name. Amen.*

O Christ, who didst come that we might have life, and might have it more abundantly, we thy disciples come to Thee, that our lives may be filled with the fulness of God. Give us victory through faith over the sin that so easily besets us, and may we with minds lighted and hearts purified feel thy love which passes knowledge. Amen.

O God, Source of life and truth, whose light is in the world around us, and in the mind of man; help us to have thy words written in our hearts. And may we not merely possess thy truth as a treasure, but may it possess us as its instruments, through Jesus Christ our Lord. Amen.

O God, Father of mercies, we pray for all victims of injustice, of fear, of want and of war. May thy spirit so move among men that those who are strong may help to bear the burdens of the weak, may help the needy and the oppressed, and banish all injustice from the world, that all people may have a chance for a good life, and that there may be peace and good will among men, in Christ's name. Amen.

For Morning

We thank Thee, O God, our Father, for the new day which thou hast given. Help us this day to be loyal to Thee, and skilful in building our home as a part of thy

* From *The Kingdom, The Power and The Glory*, p. 70, by permission of the Oxford University Press.

kingdom on earth. Be with us as we go about our duties and in thy strength may we do all things well. Amen.

For Use in Happiness

We come to Thee in our happiness, our heavenly Father, thou Giver of true joys and of all good gifts. We pour out our thanksgiving before Thee, and ask that through the experiences of life we may know Thee better, so that we may reveal Thee in our lives, and may be to others givers of help and cheer, through Jesus Christ our Lord. Amen.

For a Time of Trouble

(Before offering this prayer it would be well to read passages listed under "Marital Agreement" on page 114)

In our trouble we turn to Thee, O God; for thou art our Father and our eternal Friend. In our distress we seek thy help. In our perplexity we ask thy guidance, and as we are prone to error we ask that thou wilt give us the wisdom that we need. Be thou our strength and support. In thy light may these dark shadows pass away, and even in our time of trouble may thy grace be sufficient for us and thy love sustain us, through Jesus Christ our Lord. Amen.

For Use at Evening

O God, who by thy grace hast kept us through this day, and hast brought us to the quiet of evening; as the day is thine, the night also is thine, and we are in thy care. We pray that thou wilt accept the work that we have done today, and forgive us for those things which have been wrong. In thy peace may our cares and burdens be forgotten, and may we rest this night in Thee. Amen.

Penitence

O God, we thy children come to Thee in penitence, for we have done things that we ought not to have done, and have left undone things that we ought to have done, and we need thy forgiveness.

We pray to Thee, who art gracious and merciful, to give us a new mind, that we may turn from all evil ways, from words that ought not to be spoken, from thoughts that are alien to thy kingdom, and from deeds that are done without love; and may find new life in Thee, through Jesus Christ our Lord.

THE BIBLE IN THE HOME

The family will be enriched by reading such great passages as the following until they become a part of the mental and spiritual furniture of the home:

Beatitudes, Matt. 5:3–12

Bread of Life, John 6:35–40

Burdens, Ps. 55:22

Call of Disciples, Mark 1:14–20

Christmas Stories, Matt. 1:18–2:23, Luke 1, 2

Church Attendance, Ps. 122; Heb. 10:25

Confidence, John 14

Discipleship, Mark 8:34–38

Faith in God's Love, Romans 5:1–10

Family Influences, II Tim. 1:3–5

Forgiveness, Ps. 32

Foundations, Matt. 7:24–27

Freedom in God, Romans 8

God's Care, Matt. 6:28–30

God's Dwelling, Is. 57:15

God's Love, John 3:16

God's Ways, Is. 55

Good Shepherd, John 10:1–18

Grace, Eph. 2

Gratitude, Ps. 103, 107, 116

Great Commandments, Mark 12:28–31

Greatness, Mark 10:42–45

Guidance, Ps. 23; 32:8; 73:24

Help in Trouble, Ps. 46, 91

Helpfulness, Gal. 6:2

High Thinking, Phil. 4:8

Invitation, Matt. 9:13; 12:28; John 6:27

Justice, Micah 6:6–8

Law of the Lord, Ps. 19

Light of the World, John 8:12

Light Shining, Matt. 5:14–16

Love and Life, John 3:16–21

Love Is of God, I John 4

Love That Never Fails, I Cor. 13:4–8

Moderation, Prov. 30:8

Obedience, Ps. 119: 1–16, 33–40

Parables, Matt. 13, Luke 15, 16

Penitence, Ps. 51

Sermon on the Mount, Matt. 5–7

Spiritual Food, John 4:31–38

Telling the Children, Ps. 44, 78

Test, I John 3:24

The Shepherd Psalm, Ps. 23

True Worship, John 4:24

Truth Makes Free, John 8: 31, 32

Water of Life, John 4:1–15

Way of Blessing, Ps. 1

Wisdom, Prov. 3–5

Various Thoughts from the Psalms, Nos. 3, 5, 91, 103, 116, 119, 121, 139

MARITAL AGREEMENT

Some time before the ceremony the couple may wish to sign the following agreement:

—Recognizing that my chosen one stakes happiness on the faith that I will be the best possible life companion, I gladly agree—

—always to hold our love most precious, realizing that love is not merely a way of feeling, but an attitude of cherishing each other and meeting each other's needs;

—to be considerate of feelings, and try to put myself in my mate's place when we see things differently;

—to be courteous and fair in my speech, and whenever I have offended to ask for pardon;

—to strive to be slow to take offense, and quick to forgive, as I would be forgiven;

—to strive to add to the joys and lessen any sorrows of my mate;

—to seek fair and kind solutions for any problems that arise between us; and in case of any problem that we cannot handle by ourselves, to seek the help of a pastor or other counselor.

—to read the marriage vows again occasionally either alone or together.

All this I promise gladly and with all my heart.

HUSBAND _____

WIFE _____

As a business takes an inventory at times, so there may well be times when the husband and wife consider together the assets of their marriage, each thinking of the good points in the other. If there are unsolved problems they may well cut them down to size and put their heads together, and their hearts, to solve those that can be solved and reduce the others to manageable proportions. And as a person's health can be safeguarded by a regular medical check-up, so also there are times when a marriage check-up may be made by going back to the marriage vows and then proceeding to build up the health of the marriage in every possible way. A book or a marriage counselor may help.

Chapter IX

A MARRIAGE SERVICE

THE MARRIAGE SERVICE takes a variety of forms. The following, a modification of the Episcopalian service, is widely used in many denominations.

At the time appointed for the marriage ceremony the persons to be united shall stand before the minister, the man at the right hand of the woman, and the minister shall say

Dearly Beloved: We are gathered together in the sight of God and in the face of this company to join together this man and this woman in holy matrimony which is ordained of God, blessed by his favor, and to be held in honor among all men. Our Savior, having blessed a marriage ceremony by his presence, said that a man shall leave his father and mother and shall cleave to his wife and they two shall be one flesh. In a union of heart, mind and body they are to live in mutual esteem, forbearance and whole-hearted love for each other; they are to help and comfort each other, to provide for each other, as is fitting, in material things, and pray for each other as heirs together of the grace of life.

Then the minister shall say Let us pray. *He may use the following prayer, or whatever prayer he finds best.*

O God, our Eternal Father, Giver of the love which

binds man and woman together in marriage, bestow thy divine grace, we pray, upon these thy children that they may be truly united in this holy estate. Help them to grow to a new breadth of mind and depth of heart fitting their new relationship, that they may establish a home in which thy love for them and their love for each other shall give them fulness of joy. Be with them as they live together in this holy bond, from this time forth, and through all their days, through Jesus Christ, our Lord.

Then the minister shall say to the man, calling him by his Christian name:

———— will you take this woman to be your wedded wife, to live together in the holy estate of matrimony? Will you love her, comfort her, honor and keep her, and forsaking all others, keep you only unto her so long as you both shall live?

The man shall answer, I will.

Then the minister shall say to the woman, calling her by her Christian name:

———— will you take this man to be your wedded husband, to live together in the holy estate of matrimony? Will you love him, comfort him, honor and keep him, and forsaking all others, keep you only unto him so long as you both shall live?

The woman shall say, I will.

Then the minister shall say:

Who giveth this woman to be married to this man?

Then the father (or friend) shall say, I, *or by a sign, or by putting the hand of the bride into that of the minister, shall give her away.*

The minister, receiving the right hand of the woman, shall place it in the right hand of the man. Then, as instructed by the minister, the man shall say:

I, —————, take thee, —————, to be my wedded wife, from this time forward, for better or for worse, for richer or for poorer, in sickness and in health, to love and to cherish till death us do part, and thereto I plight thee my troth.

Then the woman shall take the right hand of the man and as instructed by the minister, shall say:

I, —————, take thee, —————, to be my wedded husband from this time forward, for better or for worse, for richer or for poorer, in sickness and in health, to love and to cherish till death us do part, and thereto I give thee my troth.

Then the minister shall say to the man:

—————, what token do you bring of your endless love and fidelity?

Then the best man or other person appointed shall give a ring to the minister and the minister shall say:

This ring is a symbol of a love which is complete, beautiful, and endless. May God help you to make your love perfect and eternal.

If desired the minister may offer a prayer over the ring, then he shall deliver the ring to the man, and the man, putting it on the third finger of the woman's left hand, shall say:

With this ring I thee wed, and with all that I am and all that I have I thee endow: in the name of the Father, and of the Son, and of the Holy Spirit, Amen.

If it is a double ring ceremony the minister shall ask the same question of the woman and she shall place the ring on the man's finger, and shall repeat the same words, as instructed by the minister.

Following this the minister shall say:

Forasmuch as ——————— and ——————— have consented together in holy wedlock, and have witnessed the same before God and this company, and have pledged their faith each to the other, by the authority that is committed unto me, I pronounce them *husband* and *wife.* Whom therefore God hath joined together let no man put asunder.

After this the minister shall say, Let us pray. *He may use this or some other prayer at his discretion, closing with Benediction.*

O God, our eternal Father, we thank thee for this sacred bond of love; and for the privileges and joys of the life which thou dost give us. Help these thy children as they bring all that they have and all that they are to this new union. As they establish a new home amid the homes of earth enfold them in thy love, guide them by thy wisdom, sustain them by thy presence and grant thy blessing on the fellowship which they have with other homes, that their home may be a true unit in thy kingdom Help them so to live in this world that they may have eternal life, through Jesus Christ our Lord. Amen.

The Benediction follows and then the bridegroom kisses the bride. If it is a church wedding the recessional begins.